Portions of this book first appeared in slightly different form in *Field & Stream,* © 1974–1987 by CBS Publications, the Consumer Publishing Division of CBS Publications, and *Field & Stream,* © 1988–1995 by Times Mirror Magazines, Inc.

Edited by Todd R. Berger
Designed by Leslie Ross

Printed in the United States of America

96   97   98   99   00   5   4   3   2   1

Library of Congress Cataloging-in-Publication Data
Tarrant, Bill.
        Gun dog training : new strategies from today's top trainers / by Bill Tarrant.
            p.   cm.
        Includes index.
        ISBN 0-89658-322-8
        1. Hunting dogs—Training.   2. Hunting dogs—United States—Anecdotes.
        3. Dog trainers—United States—Biography.   I. Title.
        SF428.5 T38125   1996
        636.7'0886—dc20   96–4924
                                                            CIP

Distributed in Canada by Raincoast Books, 8680 Cambie Street, Vancouver, B.C. V6P 6M9

Published by Voyageur Press, Inc.
123 North Second Street, P.O. Box 338, Stillwater, MN 55082 U.S.A.
612-430-2210, fax 612-430-2211

Also by Bill Tarrant

Best Way to Train Your Gun Dog
Hey Pup, Fetch It Up
Bill Tarrant's Gun Dog Book: A Treasury of Happy Tails
Problem Gun Dogs
Tarrant Trains Gun Dogs
Training the Hunting Retriever: The New Approach
How to Hunt Birds With Gun Dogs
Pick of the Litter
Training the Versatile Retriever to Hunt Upland Game
The Magic of Dogs

This book is dedicated to Dean Gordon A. Sabine, who gave me a scholarship for a master's in journalism at the University of Oregon and then a fellowship to get a doctorate in journalism at Michigan State University. I want Gordon to know the good he did through these scholarships to bring kindness to the world of dogs.

Contents

Gary Ruppel excites pointer pup with pigeon feather dance.

Introduction

Butch Cassidy and the Sundance Kid were in awe when they asked, "Who is that guy?" Not knowing for sure, they jumped off the cliff into the roaring rapids and bobbed away.

Well you can keep dry. Cause I'm going to tell you who the awesome people are in this book. They're the new breed of American gun dog trainers, and they are featured here because they fit the ideal as I see it. They fit the Tarrant Standard. Not all of them fit perfectly. But each of these gun dog trainers has one or more exceptional talents or philosophies or characteristics. If we could have all these values in one person, we'd have a Dog God.

Here's why.

1. These people train with their heads, not their hands.

2. They train with intimacy, not intimidation.

3. They position dogs to self-train.

4. They use dogs to train dogs, so any resentment the dog may have is vented against his own kind and not against a human.

5. Some of these trainers try to let pups run wild for six or eight months before taking them to a yard drill. But at least two dog trainers in this book say, "Not necessarily so." Same goes for tenet number 6 that follows. Find out why.

6. The training emphasis of many of these trainers is pen-raised and wild birds. They believe you can't train a bird dog without a bird. And if you want a lot of bird dog, you use a lot of birds. Many of these trainers even say go to birds first, and you'll have a hunting dog. Go to yard drills first and birds later, and their contention is you'll have little to nothing.

7. These trainers never place a dog in a position where he has to say no.

8. They never place a dog in a position where he can disobey.

9. They either train with sensitivity, influence handling, or bonding (these are three different but similar concepts). This requires two things:

unlimited time with the dog (or commitment) and lots of sincere love.

10. In all things the dog is the given benefit of the doubt.

11. If the trainer and the dog disagree on matters of the wild—such as, is the bird in the soybeans or the lespedeza?—the dog is always right.

12. Domination in gun dog training is dead.

13. If you train for compliance, your program will fail. If you train the dog for self-drive and independence, your program will succeed.

14. All training enhances the dog's natural ability and gives the dog total discretion in the field.

15. Ninety-five percent of all dog performance comes born in the dog. Five percent is plastered on by humans. If that dog you're training had been left in the wild, he would have learned to hunt on his own. He really don't need you.

16. Consequently, the most important thing in dog training is what you've got to train: i.e. breeding. You can't shoot 12-gauge shells out of a .22. So if it ain't in the dog, you're never gonna get it. And God puts it in—not humans. Consequently, the future of gun dogs is based on quality breeding. A hit and a lick won't do it. You've got to know exactly what you're doing.

Also, the top gun dog trainers will not breed a dog they had to train to performance. They don't want a human-made dog, they want a God-made dog.

17. Most gun dogs are superb athletes, but not all of them are smart. So breed for intelligence. Like Bob Wehle of Midway, Alabama—the world's most successful gun dog breeder—says, "I don't want a dog eighteen months old that's still a pup." And what's one way Bob checks for intelligence? He adds, "The pup in the litter that can figure out how to get through the gate is one worth considering."

18. Not one trainer in this book teaches anything that ain't needed; i.e., if it don't apply to hunting a bird, why teach it?

19. The happiness of the dog is more important than anything else. The trainers in this book produce dogs that hunt because the dogs want to, not because they have to.

20. If a dog makes you mad he's defeated you.

21. Therefore, it's more important the trainer control him- or herself than control the dog.

22. Paramount to all other tenets in the standard, you'll find that

any trainer who is a puppy person is tops in producing class gun dogs. Puppy success shows the trainer's patience, tolerance, good nature, kindness, sensitivity—all those positive things demanded of anyone who teaches.

23. To train with pain is not training at all, but senseless brutality.

24. You must learn to use the land and the effects of nature to train your gun dogs.

25. There's not a gun dog problem that can't be solved with a bird.

26. The breaking's in the breeding.

27. And as we go along, you'll be learning more requirements needed to make a great gun dog trainer, that went into making the master trainers who are featured here. And the kind of dogs that came into their lives and permitted them to break out of the pack.

BECAUSE

America's got something it never had before. The world's best gun dog trainers. People who know domination in gun dog training is dead.

Where today's gun dog prospect is let go—free to roam the hills and knock holes in the skyline and bump birds and flop on cow pies and eat dead toads.

Gun dogs of the past were too often controlled with domination, threat, and sometimes barbarism. The new gun dog is mentally manipulated with what Gary Ruppel of Parker, Colorado, calls "influence handling." What Mike Gould of Kamiah, Idaho, calls "the invisible rubber band." What the author of this book calls "bonding with FIDO."

What it all amounts to—and you'll know the system and how to use it when you finish this book—is *we now leave all the dog in the dog.*

THE PREDATOR

Consider this: God put dogs here and gave them the disposition of predators and had them live by their wits and their wild cunning, and man bridled all this to get a bird for his pot.

But in doing this man neutered the dog's spirit. He tamed his savagery—or let's say, his native wit—too much. Man took the hunt out of the dog and put in his presumptive commands to heel, sit, stay, come. Man made a mechanical dog, when what he really wanted was a natural dog to hunt for him in a natural world.

Mike Gould entices older client dogs with jetting pigeon.

AND WHAT HAPPENED?

After doing all these wrong things, man ended up taking the dog hunting instead of the other way around. Can you imagine that?

Man thought he knew that much. He told the dog to hunt here, to hunt there. He told him whoa, go, or hell no. Can you believe it? A dog that can smell a million times better than we can. A dog that can outrun us, outswim us, outlast us in cold, rain, wind, and snow. A dog that can catch sight of game, or mentally sense the impending presence of game, before it ever appears to a human. Yes, I can prove this happens, for dogs are intuitive, telepathic. Dogs can read our minds; dogs have extrasensory perception. To have a creature this amazing and nullify his best effort. Unbelievable.

So imagine our impudence when we yell over to the dog, "No, Pup, hunt over here."

Tell me why we've had training programs the past six decades that stripped the native genius from the dog? Well no more. Now our programs enhance all these qualities, all these capabilities.

It's amazing the dog ever endured us. But the charm of the animal, the grace and forbearance and gentleness and love and all those magnificent virtues God showered on the dog and gave but a drip or two to humans—must have kept the dog from biting the hand that misled him.

I like to think the dog thought, "Someday, he'll learn. We've just got to wait a little longer."

PUT IT TO THE TEST

For we know things now. We've researched things. We've taken our dogs into the laboratory of the wild and worked them one way and then another way, and, gee, we finally found out what makes the best hunting dog we can take hunting.

And what's that?

This: If you teach a pup discipline first, then take him to birds, you'll never have a hunting dog.

But if you let the pup run wild, and arrange his quests to continually keep him in contact with both pen-raised and wild birds—and then go to yard drills—you'll have a hunting dog like you've never seen. And why is this? Simple. You'll have a self-trained dog. Not a human-trained dog. *You'll have a hunting dog that learned all the things a hunting dog does out hunting.* Not a human-trained dog who learned all the things a human wants in yard drills.

We've seen it time and again; people so often want things that are totally wrong.

IT'S THIS SIMPLE

Domination in gun dog training is dead. That's what this book is about. And you may be surprised, but that just might be what the whole world is about.

For years I've asked you to be kind with your dogs—gentle, thoughtful, supportive. To give your dog the benefit of the doubt. To assume maybe you're wrong, and maybe the dog could be brought along another way. What would be that way? I've probed and beseeched and counseled and hoped that our dogs would have a better life. Because I do not want dogs hurt.

DOMINATION

So imagine my joy when I picked up the *Arizona Republic* newspaper one morning and found a front-page story saying—now get this and then we'll spend the rest of the book meeting top gun dog trainers and getting foolproof tips for your dog—"Man is confronting his ancient world view of dominion. It is a deep struggle, a way of facing the mistakes of our past. For most people, it is occurring at the subconscious or subliminal level. But it is occurring."

The columnist was John Balzar of the *Los Angeles Times*, and he was writing about America's new penchant for preserving predators. For putting wildness back in nature. *And how does that differ from putting wildness back in the dog?*

Balzar wrote, "This summer . . . the administration gave its OK to reintroduce the gray wolf to Yellowstone National Park."

Why does Balzar care about this? This is where the man gets brilliant.

He writes—and consider this in light of all we're tying to do to humanize dog training—he writes, "What is happening here is an old way of thinking [in America] in which we strived to control everything [is now being replaced with] a new, reciprocal relationship with the natural world."

Back to dog training. So much past training was based on domination in which we kicked the dog, beat the dog, shocked the dog, cussed the dog, and now we've come up with a new method based on reciprocal-empathic-response (RER). We let the dog read us through empathy, and then we study the feedback of the dog and proceed with techniques that keep this empathy positive. In other words, the trainer bonds with the animal and maximizes communication.

And what's bonding? That's when a dog and a human become one heart, one soul, one mind, one intent. When the dog and human are no longer separate entities, but one. When a look of disapproval from the human hurts the bonded dog more than if he were hit with a 2x4. That's bonding. Getting the dog to perform out of love.

Humans are no longer dogs' masters, they have become their helpmates. Also, dogs perform out of love, not fear. They hunt because they want to, not because they have to.

Author bundles pointer pup as part of bonding.

A SHAKY VOICE

Now it's hard to believe—I couldn't believe it myself—but when I finally reached John Balzar by telephone at the *Times* Seattle bureau, my voice was shaking. I was so excited I could hardly sound rational. I told Balzar this was probably the most brilliant article I had ever read. Why? Because it substantiated all you and I have been talking about and practicing for decades.

I told Balzar I must have permission to quote from his article and he said, "Go ahead."

Now what else was I after?

Balzar writes, "Several states have acted to protect the existing predators." Then he asks, "Why predators?" And asks again, "Why of all times, now?"

Then he answers, "Maybe because the frontiers are finally all gone and America's fabled self-belief in its frontier spirit is fading."

Then he quotes a husband and wife team whose mission is to explain the wild wolf to America. Bruce Weide and Pat Tucker, of Missoula, Montana, ask, "Why wolves? In a word, wildness."

Now get this. Bruce Weide explains, "You can save whales and baby seals, and you've saved animals. But if you save wolves, you've saved wildness."

Weide then says, "People are tired of thinking they can *control everything*. They don't want to live in the wild world, but they want it to be there—we hear it time and again, it gives people satisfaction to know there's something out there *free from human control*."

And suddenly I understood a big part of—ME! I understood in part why all these years I kept writing those gun dog training articles asking hunters to let the dog keep his spirit, to let the dog be an independent creature, to give him ultimate latitude with minimum control, to witness the miracle that comes when the dog gives back to you a free and wild and questing sprit. When the dog again takes you hunting, instead of you directing him. When the dog becomes an asset beyond your contribution.

I know Balzar had to think I was a nut, getting him on the phone, raving about his insight. But he says it so well. Listen. He writes, "Today, many of the causes that make newspaper headlines are about money, power, lawlessness in the cities, the whiz-bang of the future. The return of predators is the contrary: *human altruism, the relinquishing of power, the return of nature's laws to the out-of-doors* and the nostalgia for the timeless howl of the wolf."

Repeat: *Human altruism*. We're talking about that.

Relinquishing of power! America's top trainers have already done that.

The return of nature's laws to the out-of-doors. That's what we're doing now with Pup.

You and I have been doing these things for two decades, and we knew, in a sense, why we felt the way we did and why we were training our gun dogs with latitude and kindness, but did we grasp the deeper meanings?

I see it this simply.

THEN MAN MISLED THE DOG

The dog was a craftsman in the wild because he was the essence of wildness. Then the miracle happened: The dog left the wilderness and threw in with humans. And that worked.

But when humans no longer knew nature (now we're talking of the city dweller), or the rules of nature, or the ethics of the wild, they began dominating the dog, which finally ended in brutality. And that's what you and I hate, and that's what we are trying to eradicate. In other words, we've been saying all along, give us a little of that wildness back. We're tired of the mechanical dog.

We're tired of force. We're tired of being so impudent as to think we can train the dog to hunt better than his genetic disposition had him doing before history.

We've taken this dog, this product of nature, and bore down on him with human expectations. Why? Because of this mania we have deep within us for domination (especially with field trial retrievers). Well domination is gone. All gone.

How much better to see the dog's loving eyes rather than the slitted and fearful sideward glance of a dog beaten into performance.

NOW LET'S GET STARTED

We've got so many things to do. Train with love. Train more than one class of gun dog and become enriched by the crossover. Take our field trial champions hunting. Select only pros who have a dog of their own that stays in the house and rides in the pickup. Require each pro we re-

Jim Charlton and Sage share a moment of love during training session. (Photo by Betsy Charlton Powell)

tain to actually go bird hunting every season, for there's hardly a field trial pro that does. And not only do many pros not go bird hunting—there are some who don't like dogs. Well, as clients we must make sure such pros don't get our business.

Not just because these may be pros who don't love dogs. But how in the hell are they going to train your dog to hunt if they 1) neither enjoy hunting, or 2) don't know the first thing about hunting, themselves? Now that's something to think about, and I bet you a case of shells it never entered your mind before.

Yes, we're going to break all the old rules. That's the only way we'll get the new job done.

We now want to give the dog his head, his genius, his nose, his wiles, and his hunting instincts, that heretofore we idiotically muted and beat down.

There are ways to regain some of that wildness that made the dog a hunter. That made him produce more food for man than man could bring home alone. That made him so indispensable to early man's survival that the dog finally ended up under man's table and in his bed.

We're going to learn about that, too.

Pointer twirls to breakaway pheasant as Mike Gould prepares to shoot.

1

Mike Gould

The trainers selected for this book are not interchangeable parts. A Buddy don't equal a Bill equal a Gary equal a Butch. I see a standard all gun dog trainers must attain. Several of the people in this book have almost reached that ideal, some are en route, two have made it. It's a matter of the heart.

Mike Gould don't have store-bought knowledge. He learned his trade outside the public schools, away from the village square: he learned it high in the Rockies, deep in the gorges, back in the high deserts, out on the plains. Mike Gould knows gun dogs.

He knows how to train 'em and hunt 'em in every kind of cover for every kind of bird.

THAT'S MY LIFE

Over the course of forty years, I've developed a standard against which all gun dog trainers should be measured. That's the basis of this book. What's the standard, who fulfills it?

FIELD & STREAM

As gun dog editor twenty-four years for *Field & Stream* magazine, I've met most of the world's great gun dog trainers. For many years before that, I trained Labrador retrievers and competed on the classic field trial circuit.

At the big trials, and in two-dollar motel rooms each night (yes I remember one at Lee's Summit, Missouri, where the bed was firm and the floor was mopped), I was a mouse in a far corner inconspicuously listening to the pros compare their tactics and reveal their thought processes. Year after year, I was never noticed.

So I've listened to the world's best, many of them legends, explain their methods and share their goals. I've watched them train, care for, and handle their dogs. I know what these trainers are thinking (or have thought), what they're made of, what they want, and what they'll do to get it.

Among the whole of them is a handful of truly talented and kind individuals who are a credit to the world of dogs. For you see, what a dog needs most is love and self-assurance, security, if you will. I'll give you two examples.

Love is sitting beside you—you don't even know it—and when you look down, you're immediately melted by that constant, deep, and worshipful stare. Love is driving along in the pickup and gradually feeling a dog's head lean against your shoulder. You know you're needed.

Security? Take off for a week and come home. Pup does one of two things. He panics and goes nuts and leaps higher than your shoulder, or he kisses your face and scratches your legs and possibly gets a canine hung up in one of your nostrils. "Thank God," the dog is shouting, "my world is complete again."

Either that, or this: Pup does not know you. He turns from you. He sulks and eats worms. He moves sag-shouldered when he walks, he can hardly stand, his jowls flare flat to the floor, and his eyes see off to Tibet. All this means you must pay. You must hurt as he has been hurt. You must know how it feels to be insecure. To have your world uninhabited. To have the source of your life disappear.

MIKE GOULD

Mike Gould knows these things. Mike Gould knows most things. Mike Gould regards dogs as I do. They're gifts from God. He recently said to me, "How can anyone hurt a dog; they are so precious."

That's why Mike leads the list.

ANOTHER LONG TALK

We're sitting on the stoop of Mike's sun-splashed front porch outside Carbondale, Colorado, as he tells me, "You know, Bill, there's a dog above the field trial champion. And that's the hunting dog." (It's been a long time coming but Mike is now manager of the premier Flying B hunting preserve outside Kamiah, Idaho. There he has fifty-five dogs and six assistant gun dog trainers.)

Mike pauses, and I watch three Lab pups and a seventeen-month-old Arabian gelding mosey about the front yard. That's part of their training. To learn people and commotion and different settings. Sometimes the horse sticks his head in the front room when the kids leave the screen door open. The Lab pups run between the gelding's legs, and he don't kick. Mike's taught him to whoa same as a bird dog. Both the pups and the colt are some sort of marvels. As with everything Mike trains.

Mike crosses his long, thin legs—there's not an ounce of fat on him—and says, "Most of our information on what a good gun dog is comes from the field trial circuit. That's always been the standard.

"Yet, you know a field trial dog never has the opportunity to think. He knows pen-raised birds and mechanical tests and total domination by his handler. He's been taught to get a ribbon, not a game bird.

"But the gun dog knows every species of bird—if he's lucky—and every kind of cover, plus the effect of the wind and humidity and the slope of a hill. He knows where the birds hide and how they flush and where they go.

"No, Bill, there's nothing superior to the gun dog. He's the standard every hunter should use to select a pup.

"These poor field trial people . . . I feel sorry for them. I recently let them come on the property for a trial, and I sat in a lawn chair and watched. A pro came up to me and said, 'Boy this is a beautiful place . . . but you better get rid of those rocks. They're bad for running dogs around.'

"About ten minutes later a lady handler came up and said, 'Oh what a beautiful place, but you need to get rid of those trees. They block the view for the handler.'

"Then it wasn't twenty minutes until one of the judges came by—and this guy had at least a $250 aspen tree he'd just cut down—and he said, 'Boy what a great place, but you need to get rid of all that high cover down in the bottoms for we can't see our dogs.'

"And after they all left I thought, okay, no trees, no rocks, no cover.

And I realized, these field trial people are looking for a parking lot like at the mall . . . some asphalt with a little puddle in the middle. And I ask you, Bill, . . . with these interests, how could they ever produce a hunting dog?"

WHAT CLIENTS WANT

"You know I hunt big-money clients. They don't ask me if the dog's a champion. They only have one thing on their mind. Can the dog produce birds. And come to think of it—the amateur out with his dog for a day's hunt—he's thinking the same thing. Get me a bird . . . lots of birds.

"Well to do that the dog has to be a hunter. And that ain't no field trial champion."

A RETRIEVER FIELD TRIAL IS ALL WRONG

The horse stands before me, sniffing my shirt. The three pups have headed for the pond, where they'll dive for gossamer and moss, and swim after leaves floating on the surface.

Mike says, "A retriever field trial is all wrong. There's no hunting. The format says the birds have already been found, and in many cases, already shot.

"And the flushing dog trials? They make a good hunt, but that constant pattern doesn't have a thing to do with varied cover and terrain. Not if the dog has to cast for objectives.

"And pointer trial people have similar problems. Seldom is there a retrieve or the dog handled.

"Compare that to a dog just out hunting birds. A dog hunting wild. A dog that's been out there on lots of birds. And there's just no way a field trial dog can gain that expertise. There's not enough time in his life to be both a performer and a hunter.

"In order for an all-age retriever to run one of those monstrous 300-, 400-, 500-yard blinds, he must spend 75 percent of his time running blind retrieves [where the dog has not seen the bird fall]. Plus there's the trickery involved, not just the distance. The points of land scented with game birds, the suction to go ashore when swimming through a pinched hourglass of land."

Mike Gould lines up clients' Labs and calls out each one to fetch.

FORSAKE ALL HIS TRAINING

"So what does this mean? It means this. In order to run those ludicrous blinds the dog must forsake all his training on finding and flushing and fetching birds. But that's what the hunter demands. The bird. Not a blind retrieve. That blind retrieve is just a game. So the pro trainer forsakes all the things a fine shooting dog must have in order to pass mechanical tests."

WHAT'S YOUR BIRD PLAN?

"He must forsake the knowledge of all game birds, the close bonding and association, learning to hunt for the gun, learning how to keep track of each other, learning as a team how to handle each bird situation. For with grouse you have one plan, with pheasant you have a different plan. The dog needs to know all these things.

"Say a dog is a year old. He's never seen a game bird in a hunting situation. Never seen a pheasant or grouse or quail in its natural environment. So the best thing you can do is just get your gun and start following that dog and shooting birds for him.

"Stick with the fundamentals, no flimflam, good obedience, keep him happy, keep your attitude right, just show him everything about the bird and the field and the gun and every bird scenario you can imagine. And in their brain, the dog piles up all that stuff, and when he's about four or five, you've got yourself a dog far superior to any field trial dog—because your interest is in going hunting."

ON BEING KIND

"Compare this to the field trial dog that's been electronically trained from day one, and if he gets out of sight from his handler—in other words, goes hunting!—he goes into a panic, he starts hiding, or he starts coming back. But he's scared to come back so that's when he just quits thinking about the hunt at all. All he's thinking about is getting punished. [Remember, I said the handler had to be kind? Is punishment kind?] So there's no way a field trial dog can enter the field with a bona fide gun dog and compete.

"Say that field trial dog was a man. A man can't work with the boss holding a whip. He can't open up, express himself, be innovative—nothing. So the boss loses the best of the man: It's that simple.

"Yet, this dog that's never been permitted to think becomes a champion, and that's the blood the public wants for a pup. The people want the pups out of the champions. It's a Catch-22, isn't it?"

CONTROL

By now the horse has gone to the distant fields, and the wet pups have come back to soak my shirt and pants legs. Mike says, "There's a fatal flaw in humanity. Man has this latent desire to control everything. But this natural world we interface with doesn't allow for that kind of control. There's no allowance in nature for man to have his own way.

"Now let's look at this another way. Say it's August, and pheasant season opens in November. If you took a one-year-old pup and spent that time steadying him up and teaching some hand signals, you'd have totally betrayed him.

"But if you'd let him chase grouse and pheasant, and worked in all types of cover and learned how to find birds and got in the water and fell off rocks and learned how to avoid getting hurt in the logs and the forest and in the river and on and on and on . . . you'd have yourself a bird dog if you never taught him one more thing the rest of his life. *And opening day of pheasant season that pup would get you a bird.*

"We thought we had the answers when you created the hunting retriever movement, Bill. Remember, the guy showed up in his pickup at that first test hunt you judged down in Louisiana with ol' Jack in the back, a chain around his neck. Why there were two hundred entrees at that first hunt. Hunters were interested. But this domination thing. Man scuttled the concept in ten years . . . went right back to the man-made mechanical tests that make no difference to a hunting dog."

SO WHAT'S THE ANSWER?

"So what's the answer? Either these people have to train their dogs to hunt birds, or place them with a trainer who does. A trainer who's got land and birds and wants to turn out hunting dogs instead of remote-controlled robots."

The sun has passed by, heading for the west. I look at the fly-rigging leaning against the big shade tree. "Let's go fishing," I tell Mike. He sighs and says, "Can't, got to feed dogs. But you take those three pups and go on down there. If you can't catch anything . . . they probably will."

SO THAT'S MIKE

The above visit, which I first reported in *Field & Stream* magazine, introduces us to America's most brilliant and innovative gun dog trainer today. Mike is keeping all the faiths—and starting some new ones for each of us to adopt.

He's a master at training more than one kind of gun dog breed, and a trainer is enriched by such variety. Crossover training presents many unique breakthroughs, especially for those who can train both dogs and horses. Such a trainer is Delmar Smith of Edmond, Oklahoma, the man who made the Brittany a gun dog in America. Who won ten national championships with this spitfire, little breed.

For example, Delmar brought the old picket line from horses to dogs and called it the chain gang. In my estimation, for what it does, the chain

Mike works his power-bar invention. Bar is lowered across lap to turn dog right.

Vertical bar turns dog left.

Left-foot pressure on power bar prompts dog to sit and stay.

gang is the most significant piece of training equipment in dogdom.

Delmar also gave us the nerve hitch, retrieving table, and whoa post. I reported all these things in a book twenty years ago and visit few places today where I don't find them being used by America's gun dog trainers.

And that's the kind of contribution Mike has made and is making. He's given us the looking-glass drill, to help dogs run a straight line; and the power bar to teach obstinate "brought-to-the-pro" adult dogs their yard manners.

But that's not Mike's real contribution. Far from it. Mike is a dog philosopher. He thinks of what we really should be doing with our dogs and why. Mike lives nature. He knows nature. He is intimate with nature. Not on the surface, as you might think. But deep. Here I'll show you.

GOIN' FISHIN'

Mike and his oldest son, Bryce (who would later become junior national skeet champion), and I were going trout fishing some six years ago, and we were skirting a creek when Bryce said from the back of the Jeep, "Dad . . . why can't we put this stuff somewhere else so I can sit down?"

Mike yells back at him, "I never got to sit in the back seat until I was twelve."

"You lied to me then," I tell Mike, "you said you were so poor as a kid your car had no seats, and your dad drove sitting on an orange crate."

Mike grins and continues to yell above the engine's protest, "Poor! I'll tell you how poor we were. My folks were so poor they couldn't afford to have kids. The neighbors had me."

The sun glares bright, so you must squint at the landscape, the made-up fishing rods dance at an angle over the Jeep's rear end. Suddenly, the Jeep strikes a rock and leaps sideways, like a mustang, to kick the dirt bank and bounce back.

"Ho . . . ," I yell. "That rock got us."

THE MOUNTAIN SPIRIT

And this is the first time I ever hear Mike talk like this when he says, "It was the Mountain Spirit."

"The what?"

"The Mountain Spirit . . . he knocked us sideways off that rock. I don't know why, but he has his reason."

"What are you talking about?"

"You must learn to respect the mountain," Mike tells me.

"To know it is to fear it as well as love it. Each mountain has its own spirit . . . did you know that? And the Mountain Spirit . . . what he is is a maintenance man. His job is to keep his mountain in balance. Sometimes he has to make painful decisions like burning off some timber or washing out a gully.

"People come and upset the mountain's balance. Especially nowadays. So the Mountain Spirit has to fight to hold everything together. To hold it in harmony. The birds, the trees, the animals, the grasses, and yes, even the rocks. The mountain is entirely his responsibility."

I turn to look at Bryce. He's hanging on the roll bar as he listens to his dad. Mike says, "The mountain knows the way to cripple you. He knows he can knock a mirror off this old Jeep, for example. That's why they're gone.

"He can scratch the paint, even break a window, but that wouldn't slow us down. Yet, if he gets it in for you, he can stop you dead in your tracks. He sees this Jeep as a porcupine, with the one true weakness underneath. A flat tire is just a delay, but a good whack at the transfer case can put us down for the count. You don't taunt the mountain."

LIVING NATURE AND HARMONY

I was interested in going fly fishing: now I'm in open-mouth wonder at what I'm hearing. This dog trainer speaks of a living nature and of harmony. Does he have that in himself? Is that what he transmits to the dogs? Is that why they do so well?

He says, "The Mountain Spirit is not hard to find. I simply recognize his presence and formally ask his approval of our intentions.

"We may have come for grouse or a nice buck, but we will take what he gives us and go about our way. You see, he only allows us to come and go as he wishes; we are his guests."

THE DOCUMENT

Mike turns in the seat and tells Bryce, "The Spirit tells me of a gift he has given you. He has asked me to explain it, and I will do that the best I can."

The boy does not move. His eyes are walnut brown, and they carry that great wonder of a pointer pup watching you as it's standing at a kennel gate.

Mike says, "The gift is in the form of a document. This document is everything. He has placed it in the furthermost corner of your heart.

"On this document are written the laws of the mountain. The laws tell what is expected of you as you spend time here. You will never take more than your share. You will never leave litter nor deface the rocks or trees. You will always be careful with fire.

"You will forever realize the importance of addressing the Spirit as you come. You will always be grateful, even if the Spirit denies your request. You will love these animals and birds as if they were your own.

"You will try to understand the values of all involved, instead of just what concerns you. Catching a mess of fish is easy in these creeks, but keeping only what you need takes discipline; it takes devotion."

The boy does not look up. His father tells him, "The Spirit says the document is already in your heart and so it is. You may leave it there and refuse its promptings, but it will always be there. When you abuse the mountain's laws, your heart will ache with unfamiliar pain.

GLADNESS AND APPRECIATION

"As you learn moderation in all ways, the ache will turn to gladness and appreciation.

"During this phase of your life you will become more and more aware of these laws. You will begin to take pride in what you do and for the first time be a part of your surroundings. As the sense of belonging to the mountain grows, the document will grow. It will get bigger and bigger according to your ability to absorb its meaning. And finally there will come a day when the document will cover your entire heart and still another day when it fills your soul.

"As your mouth is the fountainhead by which your soul may speak, you will suddenly have the opportunity to give the gift of the Mountain Spirit to those around you. By telling others of your experiences, you will place the tiny document in the heart of many. Now . . . let's grab those rods and go fishing."

THE SPIRIT IS A LOVING ONE

The boy remains still. His dad tries to sense his thoughts. He says, "Don't be afraid of what I've said. Don't be afraid of the Mountain Spirit, neither. He has allowed us this day in his kingdom, and he has given us a great gift.

"The Mountain Spirit is a friendly one. I have known him all my life. He has given me many memories and promises many more."

MY FATHER

"Since I was born of it, the spirit is a loving one. For you see, the spirit of this mountain is also the spirit of my father who brought me here back then as I bring you here today.

"For this reason, I treasure the air I'm breathing right now. My father breathed this air, as I do, and you do, and your children will.

"But remember this well. The mountain never belongs to you. It always belongs to others. So you, too, must become the guardian, sort of

Mike jazzes up chain-gang pointers with flyaway bird.

like the Mountain Spirit's helper. Like today, it's not sufficient we just catch fish. No. We must always think of others. We must always help others.

"Today while we fish let's look for a stick. All right? We need to find one sturdy, but not heavy. We will give it to a good friend who has need of it when he walks. It will support him. But you must know this: Support comes in different ways, some physical, some spiritual, some moral."

(The stick is for me. I'm the one with the arthritis.)

GREEN-STICK PEOPLE

Mike goes on to say, "Don't pick a green one. That won't work. And why? Because it's too young and springy. Not enough experience yet to become a walking stick. A green stick like that will bend when you need it most, just like some people. You need to pick a walking stick like you would hope to find a good friend."

Bryce leaps from the back of the Jeep with his rod. He runs toward the creek, tugging up the waders two sizes too big for him, the fishing vest hanging below his hip pockets.

Mike waits for me to stand and get circulation in my feet. Then we walk out on a rock. Mike says, "That's the Roaring Fork valley down there and right over there is where the Frying Pan River comes in. Those are the mountains that make up the Elk range.

"Why you can see way above Aspen to the Continental Divide. And that there," he points, "is Mount Sopris. Between Mount Sopris and Chair Mountain is the Crystal River valley. Long before I was born, they brought marble out of there to build the Lincoln Memorial.

"Off to the west there, beneath the bright sunlight, I can just make out the canyons of the Colorado River. Do you see them?"

I nod my head that I do.

"And each of those mountains has its own Spirit," he tells me. "To set foot on any one of them, a man must ask homage."

"You're something else, Mike," I tell him. I once taught Plains Indians' Folkways and Mores at a university. I lived off and on with the Kiowa down at Rainy Mountain, Oklahoma. And I was adopted by Chief Shunatona of the Pawnee. But never have I heard a man more one with nature. Never.

Without saying another thing, we walk slowly away from the outcropping and edge down to the creek. I cast to feel a tug at my fly, and it comes involuntarily . . . I find I'm saying thanks to the Mountain Spirit.

SO WHAT?

And why did I tell this non-dog story? Well, I ask you: Would you want a man like this to train the dog you're going to take hunting? Hell, I'd want a man like this to teach my son.

Hoyle Eaton preps pointer pup and sets him up for camera.

2

Hoyle Eaton

Having come out of the traditional era of gun dog training, it's amazing how much of the standard Hoyle Eaton developed—before I set about to define it. I recall, while doing graduate work at the universities, I was told a man doesn't have ten seconds of original thought in a lifetime. Meeting Hoyle Eaton let me know all this knowledge I had accumulated was here long before me.

A bunch of chalk-eyed cowboys were draped on the corral poles at Delmar Smiths' diggins' outside Edmond, Oklahoma. Ol' Delmar was always buying "ruined," pleasure horses and putting a mouth back on them and selling them for a pretty penny. You see, a person who don't know nothing about a horse will ride the bit, and the horse will desensitize and become a runaway. He'll no longer respond to bit commands. But Delmar will resensitize these horses and make them once again valuable.

Anyway, out of the horse trailer came this would-be mustang, just raring up and cleaving the air with his front hooves, and frothing at the mouth, and looking bug-eyed. Delmar scootched through the poles and walked up to the horse. He said something to him. And the horse came down and quit his displaying, and Delmar touched his cheek, turned, walked away, and the horse followed like he wanted to put his nose in Delmar's pocket.

THE GIFT

That's the gift.

Ain't many have it.

But Hoyle Eaton does. Hoyle is now in his sixties, a blue-eyed, chunky, natural-smart dog pro who lives outside Booneville, Mississippi. Hoyle's won six Purina awards for the best bird dog of the year. That's unheard of. And he's won four national championships with four dogs (the first three mentioned below were elected to the Field Trial Hall of Fame—along with Hoyle). For those of you who want to check your pedigree papers, the dogs were Riggins White Knight, Red Water Rex, White Cloud, and Rex's Cherokee Jake.

Hoyle came from a farm family of eleven children and grew up right near where he lives today. He tells me, "When I was a little ol' boy my daddy give me an animal of some kind to call my own. You know, it's mine. Then I was raising a calf or a horse or whatever.

"I tried to train that animal to do something out of the ordinary. And the first horse he let me have, I trained that horse to do things I'd seen in the movies.

"But I didn't know anything about how to get the horse to do it. Yet I trained him to rare up and stand up there until I told him to come down. And I could make him get up on a stump with all four feet. Made him lie down and I'd walk all over him. I was about fourteen years old."

I HAD NO BOOKS

"I had no books and nobody who knew anything was living close by. And I wasn't going to let nobody see what I was doing because I was going to make that horse do something and surprise everyone. And then when I got him trained, I'd take him up to the community center and show him off."

NATURAL TOUCH

"I think I was born with a natural touch to communicate with animals. It was born in me. And I remember the first hunt I ever went on was with my granddaddy. I guess I was three or four years old. He carried me possum hunting with some hounds of his. And I can remember the thrill of that. You know he had one of those old lanterns. There wasn't many coon in that country, but we found them out cause the persimmons were ripe.

36

"Then when I was about nine, my two uncles had bird dogs, and we all met at Grandmother's for Christmas. And they started getting those bird dogs out. And those shotguns. And I looked at those bird dogs with those sleek coats and everything, and I forgot all about playing with the other kids . . . and everything else except those dogs and those guns."

GRANDMOTHER'S AT CHRISTMAS

"They said they were going hunting, and I said, can I go with you? And they said, no son, you're too little, you couldn't keep up. I said, I'll keep up, and I'll get your birds for you . . . I'll bring your birds back to you. I wanted to go bad. No . . . they wouldn't let me go.

"So I waited until they got far enough away from the house that I didn't think they'd send me back. And I caught up with them. Then they didn't make me go back. And that was my first experience with bird dogs and hunting. But it was in me, see. It was in my make-up.

"Those dogs just fascinated me to just look at them. But when they pointed and backed, I got goose bumps. I got chills all over. I loved it when they displayed fire: showed me all that intensity and desire."

SILENT KENNELS

We're standing in the rain in Hoyle's kennel yard. The dogs in the kennel runs are quiet. That's always the way you tell a good pro: silent kennels. And those kennels don't stink, as well.

I ask Hoyle, "With this gift you got, how does it help you train better than people without it?"

THE ULTIMATE TARRANT STANDARD: COMMUNICATIONS

Hoyle answers, "I'm able to get closer to my dogs. Communicate with them better."

TRAINING WITH THE HEAD NOT THE HAND

"And I don't have to use friction tactics."

COMMITMENT

"And I spend a lot of time with the dogs. Where they get to understand me. And I think that somebody who doesn't have a natural touch, they have to do more mechanical training. Maybe they have to use more force."

THAT DOG WILL EAT YOU UP

"Here, let me give you an example," offers Hoyle. "My wife and I had been to the Purina award. And we were coming back across Alabama and stopped at a service station to get some gas. And this attendant was standing here, and there was a counter there, and something behind the counter I wanted. So I started to step back there and get it, and the attendant shouted don't go back there. That dog will eat you up. Now I didn't know there was a dog back there. So I took the guy at his word.

"I walked outside and set down in a chair. I picked up a paper and was reading it while he was getting the car ready. And I wasn't paying any attention, and in a little bit, a dog came up and put his head on my leg. And I didn't think who the dog was, and I was just petting him and reading the paper. And the man got through with the car and come back and saw that guard dog and me, and he couldn't believe it. He was fascinated. And he asked me what do you do? And I told him I train dogs. He just shook his head. And I hadn't said a word to that dog."

SOME TRAINERS CAN READ A DOG'S MIND

"You have to know what dogs are saying: They are always telling you something. I can pretty well tell by their expressions. And by their body movements. I go by that a lot. The way they present themselves to me.

"My training methods are simple. I never did consider too much the technique or the method . . . as long as the dog understood what I was trying to teach him."

BIRDS

"I teach four basic commands: To come when called, to heel, retrieve, and stop on command, whoa. I do that in the yard, and the rest of it is in the field. I take these young dogs in the field, and I run them and try to get them into as many birds as I can. And when they get ready, I break them. I teach them to hold their birds and stand steady to wing and shot."

DISCIPLINE

"And when I discipline a dog it's usually not for flushing birds—doing something that he was bred and born to do—I discipline a dog for disobeying a command. If he knocks birds, I holler whoa. Then if I get after

In his go-to-meetin' hat, Hoyle shows what a pointer should look like. Check out the chest on this dog! (Photo by Joe Eaton)

him, he knows it was because he disobeyed a command. He doesn't associate that with the birds, and cause him to lose character or be afraid of the birds."

BREEDING

"Most of the puppies I get have my bloodlines in them. And I understand that blood, and I know what to look for. And consequently I have trained so many of them I take shortcuts to get the dog to be a finished product."

THE IDEAL

"Can't do it anymore, but I used to let my pups run loose until they were about six months old. Then I started running them. I run them until they get to pointing birds and holding them long enough for me to get to the end of a check cord. Then I give them some slack, and if they break, I flip them when I holler 'whoa.' And I think White Knight had to have that done twice in his whole life. And Red Water Rex never had nothing done to him. They had that natural ingredient.

"Of course you'll come across the oddball. Like Cherokee Jake. The first time he saw me on a horse, he attacked the horse. Just standing there. He thought that horse was my enemy.

"He attacked him and was making the blood fly. I couldn't get off that horse: he was trying to run away with me, and that dog was just eating him up. So I got off the horse and got hold of the dog and led him around there a while. I understood why he had done that. He thought that horse was something detrimental to me."

THE NATURAL-TRAINED DOG

"Then later up in Canada he started attacking cows. So I had a helper put a roading harness on him, and road him through a whole herd of them. For a couple of hours. And it was all over with. Then the next time I took him out, we turned him loose, and he was going through the prairie, and I found him pointing. Right out on the bald prairie. He had a pair of old prairie chickens pointed, and he was steady to wing and shot and everything. I never had to do anything more to him. He was finished. And went on to win the national championship."

I see the rain's not going to let up. We'll do no training today. So I gradually tell Hoyle goodbye and head down the country road. The gift, I think to myself. Mighty few have it. And none of them can explain what it is. But it's out there, believe me. It's real. And if you have it, you have the makings of the world's greatest gun dog trainer. Get to it.

WHAT HE SAID

It's amazing how many laws in our standard have been incorporated in Hoyle Eaton's training program for forty years.

Communications, that's one. Intuition—reading the dog's mind. And what I call FIDO—is another. FIDO is *Filling In* information and *Digging Out* reaction.

Hoyle also mentioned breeding: He knew the bloodlines and our law says no fiddlin' around. Know what you're doing in bringing those pups into the world.

Hoyle likewise touched upon a law I've yet to mention: Pup will never hear the word "No," around birds. Nothing bad can ever happen to Pup when working birds. That's why all whoa-training is conducted in the yard, away from birds. Matter of fact, "Whoa," has nothing to do with birds. Whoa means for the dog to put all four feet flat and not move an eyelash.

I especially like Hoyle's word couplet for thoughtful training. No *friction tactics,* he said. Which means Hoyle knows exactly what I'm talking about with humane and hands-off training. And he's been doing it for four decades. So far ahead of his time.

Now Hoyle may not have a dog living in the house the way I'd prefer, but he is doing something that may be just as important. He says, "I'm spending a lot of time with the dogs." That's what I call *commitment.* To me, commitment means time. Commitment and love are the cornerstones of any training program.

Hoyle further says, "Dogs are always telling you something."

He is absolutely right. Dogs are the ultimate communicators.

Live with them. You'll learn they are communicating to each other, and to you, all the time. It's just that we have yet to decipher what they're saying. We have yet to learn how they are saying it.

I've written countless times that I'll go to my grave never knowing what I've seen watching dogs talking to other dogs and to humans. But I know they do, and someday some bright young guy or gal is going to unravel everything about it, and the world will be mighty better off for it.

GIVE THAT DOG RESPECT

For one thing, it'll give the dog the respect he's always deserved. This is the brightest of all animals. He'll be known as that one day.

Something else I want you guys and gals to notice. Hoyle said he did this or that with a dog—and he only had to do it once or twice. Well that's training. And to accomplish this you must have two things going for you.

One is split-second timing. The act must occur precisely with the command.

And two, the act must be done without emotion on the part of the handler. It must be neutral. Because dogs know your moods at all times, they know your intent, and they know your regard for them.

A dog will never perform for you if he knows you don't like him. But he'll bust a gut to keep a bond, to keep the trust, to keep a friend.

A TELEPHONE CALL

I read what I'd written about Hoyle and decided I'd call him to ask if he had some updated info he'd like to impart.

He said, "It'd just be old info about puppy training."

Now remember, up front I said the ultimate criterion of a good gun dog trainer is how well he trains a puppy.

Well Hoyle whelped White Knight in 1959, and Red Water Rex in 1962. Which means within three years he brought to life and trained and handled two pointers to the National Bird Dog Championship and membership in the Field Trial Hall of Fame.

Talk about a puppy man! As Hoyle recalls, "I hand-groomed those babies. Raised them and was with them every day of their lives."

Hoyle continues, "You got to get to know a pup before you start training. Know his temperament, things like that. After about six weeks of training I can tell what it'll take to finish that dog. The type of training and method and so forth you can use on that particular dog."

That's imperative for the new breed of gun dog trainer. To make a system fit the dog, instead of make the dog fit a system.

Hoyle continues, "I use praise a lot, I don't intimidate them, I don't confuse them . . . and if any of that occurs, I pack it up and start again.

"And when the dog becomes comfortable with me, then he'll proceed to train. Right real fast after he learns I'm not going to hurt him and I'm just trying to teach him something.

"And it's like you say, Bill, a scowl from a bonded handler has more effect on a dog than physical punishment."

"Well that's great to hear," I tell Hoyle, "for that's the way I've found it." Then I ask, "Any parting advice for the amateurs who want to train up a sure 'nuf good gun dog?"

"Yea, tell 'em to take those pups for long walks, get around people, create a bond. Expose them to all types of lawn mowers, vehicles, rackets of all description. Everything that might scare a pup. And if possible, let 'em run loose. I used to let mine run loose for months but can't any more. That's what civilization does to you."

I tell Hoyle, "I know," and I say goodbye and put the phone on the receiver. I look about my office, hear the chatter of passers-by. Yes, I repeat, that's what civilization does to you.

For I remember ol' momma dog coming in from the fields with her new litter after three months absence. All the pups pointing, backing, hunting, fetching. It's difficult to do things right all cramped up the way we are now. But that's the hand we're dealt, and we've got to play it out.

I suppose we ought to call it some type of infernal poker, where the pots go to where it's not worth the playing.

Golden retriever specialist Jim Charlton with crackerjack Sage. (Photo by Betsy Charlton Powell)

3

Jim Charlton

Jim's been training gun dogs thirty years and has the unique specialty of golden retrievers. He's presently in transition from traditional training to the ideals expressed in this book, and I'm glad to have him along. Though he had most of these ideals when I met him. Jim will make a great new-way dog trainer, for it's a matter of the heart.

I've been down many a road for *Field & Stream,* gathering gun dog stories, and all of it's been fulfilling, enjoyable. But there have always been three pitfalls: 1) Every place I visit is so beautiful I want to move there; 2) Every man (or woman) I meet would make the best of friends, yet I may not see them again for ten years; and 3) I want every dog I see.

Should I have actually brought all those dogs home, I'd now be standing at some intersection advertising with a cardboard sign, "Will scoop kennels for dog food."

So it is I pull into Jim Charlton's long, winding drive that leads me to Charlton Kennels on Sauvie Island, just twenty minutes from Portland, Oregon. A man dressed in denim angles toward the car the way old hounds approach: slow and self-musing. Then he stands there. All six-foot-six-inch stretch of him.

I'M GOING TO HAVE A GOOD TIME

I squeeze out the crack he leaves for the open car door and raise my head to greet him. I can tell on sight he's thoughtful, kind, and gentle. It's that sixth sense I've picked up from the dogs, and I know I'm going to have a good time. In five minutes, I learn Jim Charlton is a rarity in today's gun dog world. He trains all types of retrievers, but his specialty is goldens. I know no other trainer with this distinction.

I ask him why.

But he's not one to answer fast. Instead, we mosey toward the southwest, heading for a weathered hut of a place. And when I'm near enough to see, there are moss-covered deer antlers festooned on the lichen-green siding, then the door is eased open, and I enter The Charlton Duck Club. There are old wicker creels hanging there, a dusty, stuffed cock pheasant forever trying to climb away from a long-ago gun, a smattering of outdoor poetry, some dried flowers, a couple of decoys, some vintage duck stamps. Just a mishmash of stuff a bunch of duck hunters consider high-style decorating. Already I want to move to Sauvie Island and join this club.

I glance through one door and then another to finally be confronted with a sign in a bathroom that tells me, "Complaints have been registered concerning the cleaning of ducks in the toilet bowl. Please use the shower. Have a good shoot. Jimmy"

I'm beginning to understand this cypress-tall dog trainer.

THE SHOOTING FIELDS

Now Jim and I are walking toward the shooting fields. Those rows and rows of corn and Sudan grass and millet Jim plants to feed the migrating waterfowl, then floods in the fall. He says, softly, "My folks settled this island several generations back. I'm grateful to have inherited what land was left, but I'm only a caretaker for God. I'll only have it for a while and then must pass it in good order to the next guy coming along."

COCKTAIL-HOUR ECOLOGISTS

He is silent for a moment then adds, "Those cocktail-hour ecologists are always discussing what should be done with Sauvie Island. I think we've done damn good with Sauvie Island, and they should just leave it alone. If they took away duck hunting, I don't think I could afford to plant that much seed for these birds. And I have to pump water. None of this is harvested for ourselves; it's not for sale. How many thousand waterfowl are fed to fly on, but only a handful are brought to the table?"

I'm already understanding why Jim trains goldens. They're the most

Jim runs a duck club, so his goldens must hit water. And they do, better than I've ever seen before. (Photo by Betsy Charlton Powell)

mellow gun dog we have. Every time I hunt with a golden there's an urge to croon "Moon River," eat Philadelphia cream cheese, and snuggle under chamois sheets. The dogs are that *simpatico*, that laid back. But don't let that pliability mislead you. Sturdy of mind and hard of frame, they are. Fit companions for the long haul, from the rugged pleasures of the bird field to the silent lives shared in the same dirt through eternity.

CHARLEY

That happened here. Jim says, "See that?" By now we've walked west of the shooting grounds, and I turn to see the duck blinds, but at our feet there's a grass-shrouded plaque. Jim points to the grave and says, "This golden never run a trial and never won a ribbon. All he did was retrieve. I don't know how many hundred ducks he fetched off this farm. He was the finest golden retriever I ever owned."

Then Jim hesitates, thinking for a minute, before reading the inscription on the plaque. It says, "Competent, faithful companion, one hell of a fine retriever. Thanks Charley, we miss you."

Jim's voice fades off.

I gulp.

Then Jim points next to Charlie's grave and says, "There's a duck hunter buried there. He was a member of the club, and he knew Charley. He saw Charley work. He tested his credentials and received the old dog's love. So before he died he told me, 'Bury me next to Charley.' And there he lays."

I gulp again.

Finally, I say, "About these goldens, Jim—why did you take to them?"

A JUST APPRAISAL

"Oh," he says, "most of the time I've seen Labs outperform goldens. But that's not the point. The point is a lot of my best times are spent just buddying with the dog. Old Charley he rode on the tractor with me. That's what made him deaf. It didn't affect his hunting, but he did go deaf. If you want a buddy who can also fetch you a duck, get a golden. That's why I like them. They make good friends."

I know what Jim means. The golden is a happy dog; he has just enough spaniel in him to make him want to please. He's the gun dog for the man who wants to hunt both ducks and upland game, have a dog to share his bed, raise his kids, and lay in the front yard while he mows the lawn.

I once wrote, "The golden is so gentle and so biddable he is the favored retriever for ladies on the field trial circuit." I stepped on some macho toes, for several men cried foul, saying, "A golden is a man's dog." I don't think these stalwarts ever got the point. The golden is everybody's dog—infant, kid, man, woman, grandma, everyone.

There is no impugning the golden's credentials. He was the first retriever to win the National Retriever Championship in America. The year was 1940, the dog Rip, and the owner a real estate tycoon named Paul Bakewell III of St. Louis, Missouri.

PRETTY BOY

So this dog will get your duck and win you a trial, but that's not why he's popular. Oh, no. It's that beauty, that mahogany- or wheat-colored coat, rich and luxurious, highlighted by the sun. And the noble head; the deep-brown, sensitive eyes; a great skull; thick legs; deep chest; strong, feathered tail. Plus that softness and gentleness, with which he can carry a baby peep in his mouth for hours then present it to you unruffled, warm, and comfortably alive.

There's no prettier dog in the world, nor one more affectionate and caring of the guy or gal who takes him for life. He's a favorite among the Seeing Eye–dog people, the dogs for the deaf, and the incapacitated. He's also a bomb dog, a dope dog, a contraband dog. The golden's got a nose.

UPLAND GAME

Traditionally it was always said the golden was the best of all upland game retrievers. But then it was seen some specimens of the breed could hit water as hard as a Lab and stroke as fanatic as a Chesie.

But by now Jim's started talking. He says, "The major problem with a golden is he thinks too much. And sometimes gets in trouble for doing it. But the nice thing about a golden, he has more human characteristics than any other breed."

SHOW DOGS

"But there's a problem today with show breeders. They outnumber us field people ten to one, maybe twenty to one. To find a well-bred hunting golden you have to be careful, or you'll end up with one of those show dogs that can't find their way in out of the rain. We see a lot of those."

"Well," I ask, "how does a guy tell the difference without looking at papers?"

"In the northwest," Jim tells me, "the goldens are darker in color than the show stock. Almost Irish-setter red is my dog. And that goes back to Yankee's Smoke'n Red Devil, who threw a lot of field trial champions in this country. Even had one litter with four field trial champions in it.

"But the show goldens have a lot of coat problems because the fanciers are trying to breed such a light-colored dog. They seem to almost want a palomino color.

"Now field goldens are dark in color, like I say, but they are also a little lighter in the frame. But that's not to say there aren't some light-colored field goldens. There are a few. And you can also tell the difference by the feathering. The show dogs have real long hair, plus a short muzzle and square, blocky head. Why, the mouth is so short you wonder how they could hold a goose. A retriever has got to have a decent muzzle on it to hunt."

As the day passes I learn Jim's boarding kennels are full (he has flowers on the wall beside each door). He will only custom-train eight retrievers at a time and already has ten on hand, and he doesn't necessarily raise puppies. So Jim doesn't need your business, not even for the duck club. I guess, then, if you wanted to get in touch with him, it would be to reserve a burial plot.

CONTINUED

Now Jim said two things above that caught my ear and my interest. He said, goldens think too much. It takes a discerning man to see this and to know this. I'm not talking about goldens, per se. I'm talking about dogs. If they're bright, all dogs think too much.

Jim also alluded to the golden being human. Again, all dogs are nigh human. If given a chance. If recognized for their sensitivity and unique brilliance.

All of this means Jim is a discerning trainer.

Also, Jim's trained three decades by the age-old method and only recently came into contact with a gang of space-probe trainers who have adopted this new Tarrant standard. Not that they call it that. Nor that Tarrant developed all of it. Heck, these very people we are reading about were the innovators and the contributors. Major contributors.

Year after year I was in constant contact, me to them and them to me, and most of us to each other—or my going down the road and telling one what the other was doing—and that's how the standard developed. The trainers in this book did the ground work. I contemplated the naval lint. I was the pamphleteer. In this regard, Jim once told me, "Tarrant, you just delivered dogdom's Sermon on the Mount."

A MAN READY FOR ANYTHING NEW AND GOOD

Jim impressed me greatly that first day I spent with him. He was open minded, he was willing to listen to it all and measure the results, and he was flexible enough to say he would try it for the sake of the dogs.

A DOG OF HIS OWN

I want you to note one major exception with Jim that's not seen with many trainers—especially pro trainers. Jim has always had a dog of his

Sage points pheasant in brush pile. (Photo by Betsy Charlton Powell)

own. Charley was one. Today it's two golden males named Sage and Paige. They are with Jim every waking moment.

Only with this kind of association with a dog will you ever make the breakthrough in perception necessary to know what this book's method is all about. And I repeat, many dog pros do not want a dog of their own.

One of America's most widely respected and revered dog trainers hasn't had a dog in the cab of his pickup, nor in his home, for thirty years.

If a man has never known the bonded love of a dog, if he doesn't need that sense of fulfillment only a dog's love can give, then I'm sure not going to leave my dog in his care. I don't want his indifference to rub off. For the dog will know.

I don't want my dog to ever meet anybody who doesn't afford him his due. I always want my dog living in a world where he feels he's as special as he is.

OUCH THAT HURTS

And the other sore point with me: There's not all that many professional field trial trainers who hunt birds. You're going to leave your dog with these people so they can teach him to hunt, and hell, the trainer doesn't even hunt, himself. Seems unlikely such a trainer's kept up with what's needed. Right?

Well Jim not only has his own dogs with whom he's bonded, he's also one heck of a hunter. Not just birds, but elk and what-have-you. That's why Jim Charlton can take up a new oar, even get in a new boat, to finish his journey. His journey is the betterment of dogs. Not for him to make a living. But for the dog to have a life. Jim has no ego he must walk around.

AND SOMETHING ELSE

Remember Mike Gould in chapter 1 talking about the shooting dog above the field trial champion? Well this was Charlton's Charley. Jim says above, "This golden never won a trial, and he never won a ribbon. All he did was retrieve. He was the finest golden retriever I ever owned." For no other reason than this, Jim belongs on the space-probe team.

And one more thing. Remember Jim talking about the seed he planted, the birds he fed, the majority of which flew to Mexico? That's another requirement of the standard. Giving back more than you take. Conserving the game you hunt, for everything connected with gun dogdom is your abiding love.

CONSERVATION

Conservation and replenishment of game is an obligation for both the trainer and the client-hunter. But since the trainer usually owns rural land, he is therefore in a much better position to fulfill a contribution.

We want our trainers doing just that.

IT WAS THERE IN THE MAIL

And finally, those who read my books know I take them along with me. If I had read something funny or appropriate in this morning's paper, I'd of shared it with you by now.

Well, to that end a letter came today. It's from a woman, a dogman's wife, who had this to say:

"I am enclosing a photo which was inspired by your article about Jim Charlton."

Okay, what this gal's talking about is the first part of what you read above which originally appeared in *Field & Stream*.

Nanci Lien, that's this letter-writer's name, continues, "When we first read your article, our golden, Scout, was six months old and my husband, Dan, was looking for a trainer. I was raised in a household with a father who did not hunt and who was anti-gun. So although I loved dogs dearly, this whole hunting ritual was very foreign to me when I married Dan two years ago. I was not happy with the idea of sending my new puppy away for eight weeks of training, but reluctantly agreed after Dan managed to get her into Jim Charlton's 'golden retriever school.'

"Living just west of Seattle, the trek to Sauvie Island takes about four hours. Dan was not looking forward to making this trip the last four weekends of training so I agreed I would go with him at least once. That was before we dropped Scout off and saw Jim's farm.

"Your article described it perfectly. We instantly fell in love with the farm and the island and couldn't wait until it was time for us to start training with Scout.

"Over the four-week period that Jim used to transfer the dog's respect to the owners, he also, without knowing it, converted me. I began to understand the natural instinct of the dogs to retrieve and how they lived for this sport. By the end of the four-week period, I was picking up dead pigeons. No problem!!!

"I also gained a tremendous amount of respect and fondness for this man who his daughter describes as a cross between Jimmy Stewart and John Wayne. Jim is very spiritual and at peace with who he is and why he is here. So few of us ever reach that place in life.

"So I thank you, Bill, for helping us find a trainer and a friend. We are forever grateful for our '14KGLDN.'"

WHAT'S THAT STRANGE CODE?

What Nanci's doing here is calling out her personalized license plate. For you see the title to the article about Jim in *Field & Stream*, was "14 Karat Golden."

So before leaving Jim and catching up with another accomplished gun dog trainer, let's think a moment about Nanci's letter.

One pro trainer with a dog of his own. (Photo by Betsy Charlton Powell)

OWNER INVOLVEMENT

She points out some imperatives for a gun dog trainer. He must bring his client into the field and transfer the dog's allegiance to the owner, and show the owner exactly what the trainer has done to train the dog, and have the owner prove he can do the same, and handle the dog as well.

That's vital. That's demanded. A trainer who doesn't do these things leaves off the most important part of his service.

NO MORE ANTI-GUN

Also, Nanci reveals the trainer can accomplish so much with the client and the client's family in fostering shooting sports, and in teaching (without being formal about it) the mysteries and magic of the field, and reveal what Genesis means where it is written, "And God blessed [male and female] and God said unto them, 'Be fruitful and multiply, and replenish the earth, and subdue it, and have dominion over the fish of the sea, and over the fowl of the air, and over every living thing that moveth on the earth.'"

Only upon meeting Jim Charlton did Nanci know what Genesis meant, and what it held for her. Only by meeting Jim Charlton did you and I get one more comrade in our Hunting Corps.

The anti-hunters can harass you and me, but never a young lady standing there with a gun. Ho ho!

Good going, Jim.

Bimbo and Angie West with Lab pup.

4

Bimbo and Angie West

Bimbo and his wife, Angie, are the huntin'est gun dog trainers in America. That's perfect in my way of thinking: who better could turn out a sure'nuf hunting dog? And another thing: they've got so many dogs in their house there's hardly room for Bimbo and Angie. From my own living arrangements, I can tell you it keeps a couple close when there's six dogs in the bed.

Don't laugh, but before the world of women's lib we used to call them he-men. Bimbo West is that sort. He rode bulls and barebacks in rodeo for thirteen years—and that takes a man tough enough to survive in Monument Valley by just eating rocks.

Then Bimbo met Angie and fell in love. When he proposed, he knew this would be the time to get things straight. So as a he-man would, Bimbo told Angie, "Now you got to understand this. I like to hunt and fish. I like to hunt and fish a lot. So whenever I tell you I'm going—you can go if you want—but don't tell me I can't go."

They were married.

One day Bimbo came home to find Angie loading the black Labs into the wagon, and Bimbo asked, "Where you going?"

And Angie told him, "I'm going to south Louisiana to hunt geese for three days."

"But I can't go," complained Bimbo.

Then Angie told him, "Bimbo, I like to hunt and fish. I like to hunt and fish a lot. So whenever I tell you I'm going—you can come along if you want—but don't tell me I can't go."

So welcome to the outdoor world of Angie and Bimbo West of Leesville, Louisiana, who we're visiting today as they judge the started stake of the Hunting Retriever Club's tenth anniversary running near Ruston, Louisiana.

They're an affable couple, supportive of each handler, liberally judging each pup, being present not only to help the club and provide a service to the handler, but to have fun as well. For everybody's laughing, and the dogs are up and doing good, and it's all very refreshing and upbeat. As the Wests are with everything they do.

Bimbo tells me, "From our first date, Angie and I have never missed a day together in eighteen years of marriage, except when I was working the offshore oil rigs. But then we made up for it.

"We were once out hunting from October to February of the next year, and we never spent two nights in our house. The rest of it was spent camped in the woods. We bowhunted for deer, then we gun hunted for deer, we quail hunted, we duck hunted, we stayed in our travel trailer for the better part of three months. But two days we did go into town to shop for Christmas."

Bimbo is built for stout, coming in at 220 pounds for five feet eleven inches, while Angie is a slip of a girl standing five feet two inches and weighing 115 pounds. But Bimbo says, "In the woods, she outwalks me. And I'm outdoors every day as a pro retriever trainer, but Angie must sit at a desk as a receptionist in a prison. Still, she's always in shape."

I ask them, "Is there any part of your life that's not centered around hunting and fishing?"

"No," I'm told fast, "that's all we're set up for. Just look at our stuff. We've got a pickup with a four-wheeler in back; we own our own house, have a fourteen-foot aluminum boat. I drive a Jimmy; we have five dogs of our own that all live in the house; and we keep a 2,600-acre lease in Texas for deer, turkey, and lots of quail. Plus, Angie and I run a hunting lease right near our house that's 8,000 acres. It's a hunting club. And then we've got 600 acres of land leased that surrounds our house. Plus our home and pasture border game management areas. So we have lots of birds."

Then Bimbo says, "I never got to go to college, but the two of us put Angie through."

"That's great," I respond. Then I ask, "Tell me, how did the two of you meet? In the woods somewhere?"

Bimbo laughs and says, "No, we met in church, and we went on a date soon after. I had my right leg in a cast from a car wreck, and I had to drive with it resting on the passenger's seat. So Angie had to sit by the window. But the thing is, right from that first date Angie and I have never been apart for a day, except when I was on the oil rigs."

I say, "With all your weekends in the woods, I don't imagine you get to church much anymore."

And Angie's quick to respond, "Yes we do. But not to the church you may be thinking of." Then she asks, "Isn't there a church outdoors? Sure is," she answers, "sitting right there in that duck blind, or sitting right there in that deer stand. And it's sitting right there by that tree when that squirrel goes through. Yea, it sure is."

Since she's doing the talking, I ask, "Angie, it's evident you're an outdoors woman. So tell me, what advice do you have for the gals in America who are married to habitual hunters?"

She says, "I'm just a person who would never take something like that away from him—or any man. Because I've done it, and I know the feeling of hunting. I don't know what to tell a woman who's never done it. That's never experienced it. Because if she hasn't, you know, she doesn't realize what she's missing. And the thing I can say, there's a lot of women who get upset because their husbands go hunting, but they don't really understand.

"Women don't know what they're missing," she continues. "I like the outdoors. I like nature. I'm not a mall person, never have been. Going and sitting on a pond fishing does something for me I can't describe. I can't really answer it. I like the woods, I like nature, I like seeing the animals . . . I don't know."

"But what about the shooting?" I ask. "Maybe some women don't like that."

Angie explains, "I was raised with dogs and hunting. Shooting is part of it. But my sister was, too. Yet she is a mall woman. That's not to say she doesn't like the outdoors. But she likes nice things. I don't wear makeup or fancy clothes when I'm out there. I like to get dirty. I like to get sweaty. And that doesn't appeal to a lot of women."

Left: *Bimbo sets up bobwhite and woodcock pointer to fetch a water retrieve.* (Photo by Angie West)

Below: *Pointer wheels about with dummy and heads back pushing water.* (Photo by Angie West)

Pointer delivers to hand and Bimbo tells him, "You're the greatest." This is the first pointer to ever pass a test hunt started by the Hunting Retriever Club. (Photo by Angie West)

I turn to Bimbo, who is the first man to ever train an English pointer to pass a Hunting Retriever Club starting test, and ask, "Bimbo, you talk about your dogs being such a big part of your life. Tell me about it."

"Oh yes," says Bimbo, "Our four grown Labs and Hank, our lemon pointer, live in our house. Some people may not agree with that, but the more I'm around them, the more they learn. And the more I learn from each of them.

"Even when I'm sitting in the living room watching TV at night, we're training. Because . . . repetition trains dogs. And I'll tell them to sit, stay, heel, that sort of thing.

"Then when Angie starts cooking we tell the dogs to go to their spot. And that dog has to go there and sit and stay until the dog food bowls are filled and placed out. And then we go sit sometimes on the couch and make them sit there two or three minutes before we let them eat. We tell each of them individually to eat.

"Plus, the dogs have done so much for me personally. Like *they've introduced me to a better class of people.* That's what I call old die-hard hunters. The person that's just addicted to hunting, okay? Plus people invite Angie and me to go on some really nice hunts. Not because they want us, but they want to hunt over those dogs of ours."

Then Bimbo adds, "The dogs give Angie and me some real nice training sessions. *Used to be the Hunting Retriever people would meet and train somewhere. Guys would come to Louisiana from Colorado, Ohio, and other far-off places. And they'd all bring wild game from their freezers. We might spend ten days camped out, running dogs all day and eating like coons at night. It was real fun.*

"Then we hunt our dogs a lot right around the house as well as over in Texas. At the house, Angie and me and a friend hunt woodcock about every night in season. With my two-year-old pointer, the one who passed the retriever test, we shot ninety-five woodcock this past season.

"Then we went to Texas and shot three hundred quail over him. That's the way to train a dog: hunting.

"We used to do it all formal, you know. The pointer would point, we would shoot, and the retrievers would fetch. But no more. Now the pointer does it all . . . and the retrievers do it all, too. We made all-purpose dogs out of both breeds.

"But our lives are not all waterfowl and upland game bird hunting," explains Angie. "After the retriever-test season is over we go turkey hunting. And then it's off to Toledo Bend [on the Louisiana-Texas border] for white perch and bass. After that we've got to get the place ready by planting brown top millet for dove. It turns out June, July, and August are the only months we're not hunting."

So that's it sportsmen and sportswomen. A visit with a typical American couple, right? Oh you say, Bimbo and Angie spend more time in the woods than you do. Well Bimbo and Angie spend more time in the woods than Daniel Boone did. How sweet it is.

A CONTINUATION

Bimbo and Angie are so casual that some points they just made about dogs and dog training may have seemed to be no-big-deal. But they decidedly are.

Consider:

1. The dogs are central to their lives. That's how it should be. Or at least, that's the ideal. "We might spend ten days camped out," said Bimbo,

"running dogs all day and eating like coons at night." You had that much fun, lately?

That's why I have written so many times in so many places you must belong to a gun dog training club. But join and attend for the training sessions, never the politics.

2. Bimbo and Angie have five dogs themselves, and they all live inside. Note what Bimbo says: "The more I'm around them the more they learn. And the more I learn, too."

I've learned more about gun dogs by living with and constantly monitoring and everlastingly studying my six house dogs than I ever learned in the field. They, for example, are the ones who taught me so much about dog communications.

3. Bimbo said it all when he was talking about shooting woodcock at home and bobwhite over in Texas. He said, "That's the way to train a dog: hunting." We've proven that up front and will again here, and more in the pages ahead. That's the most important part of dog training: hunting. Don't overlook it. Become religious about it. Do it.

4. Bimbo has bettered his capabilities around gun dogs by crossover training. Now his retrievers hunt, and his pointers fetch. He said, "We made all-purpose dogs out of both breeds."

You know how important this statement is? The future of the gun dog is the versatile performer. Why? It costs to keep a dog. Who can afford two? Even the cars are too small to transport them. And our homes have no backyards. Plus there's all those CC&Rs—you know, the restrictions that say you can't have a dog at your place, or you can have one but he can't be more than fifteen inches tall.

So to get around all this, the dog that can do everything in the hunting field is the dog of the future. Bimbo will be ready. Will you?

5. Like Jim Charlton with his duck club operation and his beloved goldens, Bimbo and Angie plant food for the birds. To attract them, for sure, but also to sustain them. Jim Charlton told me once, "We never shoot a duck leaving the club. They've had their fill and earned it, and are entitled to take their meal back to the refuge."

Bimbo and Angie say, "We plant our fields for game feed; brown top millet is our favorite." Sure they harvest a minor number of the visiting birds—the birds who come for a hand-out. But literally thousands are

Bimbo's six-month-old Lab pup fetched thirty dove—all that were shot by a large party—on last week's dove shoot. He saw one other dog make a retrieve and then took over. (Photo by Angie West)

sent on their way with a full belly.

It's so important sportsmen and -women give back more than what they take.

6. You saw Bimbo and Angie skylarking, having a good old time at the test hunt. This is so needed. Everybody gets too serious at these things. The long faces with set jaws act like they were attending open-heart surgery instead of a dog outing. Loosen up, let your dogs have fun, and you have fun, too. And by the way, stay away from that "hostility bar" at the end of the day. Your dog deserves a safe ride home.

7. Later I asked Bimbo what he felt was important in bringing a pup from the whelping box.

He told me, "Socializing. That's what. First thing you got to do is go on walks around the place, across the creek, through the ditches. And walk the woods. Get that pup into as many different smells as it's going to come across during it's hunting life.

"Then if there's any kind of event in town take him to it. Like a rodeo parade, or a homecoming parade, softball game. Any place there's commotion and lots of people and different sounds and smells. You know people clapping and shouting and the band playing. All that.

Bimbo was studying on this when I asked, "Can you let your pups run loose? Get after wild birds on their own?"

"No, not at first. You see I want to get the obedience into them so they'll do what I tell them when they're out in the field.

"Now there's no better way to train a pup than wild birds. You can start them on tame birds . . . but don't stay on them long. Because dogs work them different than they do wild birds. And it's best to let the pup run in a pack, or with a real good older dog. Nothing can teach a pup to hunt like a real good old dog.

"What I really like to do," reveals Bimbo, "is have a pup going on seven months or so, let's say, and take him to our Texas lease for the opening of bobwhite season. You see two men with four dogs would be lucky here in Louisiana to find five coveys a day.

"But over in Texas we'll kick up twenty-five coveys in a day.

"That's why I can say . . . I took my lemon pointer over there with an older dog this past season and after a three-day hunt, he came back a bird dog. He got to work so many birds.

"Yep," said Bimbo, his mind trailed off, for I could see a faraway look take over his eyes, "That's the way to make a bird dog. Three days in west Texas."

He was studying about Texas when I left him. I can see it all so clear. You know! A lemon-and-white pup in the mesquite, cactus, and greasewood, pointing one covey after another all day. I wish I had been with Angie and Bimbo.

Bob Sprouse and Irishman holding forth in their Tennessee cabin.

5

Bob Sprouse

All men can't be hewers of wood and bearers of water. Some must sit and serve. With his backbone severed by shrapnel in the prelude to the Battle of the Bulge during WWII, Bob Sprouse returned home to contemplate a dogman's life without the ability to walk. Learn how Bob found his niche and accomplished as much for dogdom as any man who ever outwalked a Jeep.

Bob Sprouse is the national repository of the history, lore, and legend of the red setter. That mahogany- and chestnut-colored gun dog with the sun-glittered feathers (that's the dogman's name for long, dancing hair) you now see coursing the bird fields with a smooth gait, a happy countenance, and a sturdy body.

No longer is the Irish setter ruined for the bird field by the bench enthusiasts. No. He's now been bred back to functional conformation with a deep heart girth, a stacked pelvic drive muscle, protruding bones over the eyes to knock away stubble, high toenails so they won't split, a tight foot so it won't splat, a full-bored nose, and a yen to hunt.

Yes, the red setter is back. American gun dog men are the benefactors. And Bob Sprouse has the story of how it was all done, in which he never mentions his own contribution. You see, Bob is editor of *The Flushing Whip,* the national bulletin of the Red Setter Club. He's been the club's scribe since 1978, and I've always enjoyed his articles.

I'm with Bob at his Cypress Inn, Tennessee, cabin. We're so far in the sticks a camera on a satellite working with a bloodhound and an Indian scout couldn't find us. Bob rolls his wheelchair close, and this, naturally,

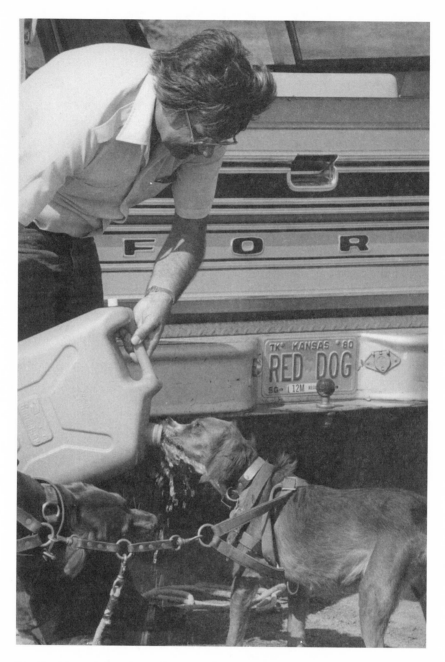

Don Beauchamp believes in roading to condition his string.

takes effort. He's now been in that wheelchair fifty years. Three of his red setters follow him, standing up to place their front paws on his legs when the chair stops rolling.

Bob Sprouse says, "My grandfather, Charles Gallagher of Logan County, Ohio, and my great uncle Pete Gordon, from the same place, had red setters back in the 1870s. They'd take the dogs to Frankfort, Kentucky, in the fall to hunt quail, and I'd tag along. It didn't take long until I talked them out of a puppy.

"In the mid-1930s, grandfather probably had the last dogs with the Campbell strain in them. Two Spring Hill, Tennessee, brothers, George and Milton Campbell, started this line of red setters—called them native setters—and that's how they registered them in the Field Dog Stud Book in Chicago, Illinois.

"Now these Campbells sent for an Irish setter from the British Isles, and they bred him to a bitch they had, and come up with a pup named Joe Junior. Joe won the Championship of America in 1884, down at Florence, Alabama, against the most famous bird dog of the day, the English setter Gladstone.

"Even back in granddad's time the Irish setter had been destroyed by the bench enthusiasts. The dogs couldn't hunt anymore; they were made for show, not work.

"Now I went into the Army in 1941," says Bob, "and when I left home I had a real good Irish setter male. When I got out of the army hospital in 1947, he was seven years old and I looked for a bitch to breed him to, but no litter produced anything. The Irish setter, as a hunter, was gone.

"Then a man named Don Waters became game commissioner in Ohio and helped create the Killdeer Plains. In 1962, one of the early red setter trials was run there, and Waters was present. He wrote and told me how good things worked—you see he was an English setter man—and he got me Marge Moffat's name. She was secretary of the Red Setter Club at that time. I wrote to her and started receiving the news.

"A couple of years later I bought my first LeGrande red setter. Now let me tell you about LeGrande and his friends who brought the red setter back. Ned LeGrande was from Virginia, and his family owned the Gudebrod fly line company when the lines were made of silk. Rusty Baynard ran a filling station in Delaware. And Arch Church was a banker or broker and lived in Pennsylvania or New York.

"Anyway, the three of them met independently at an advertised Irish setter AKC field trial in New England. And after watching the dogs run, LeGrande made the remark, 'Somebody's got to do something about the Irish setters.'

"And the three of them took it from there. They did a lot of advertising all over the country, asking for red setters that could hunt. And they had dogs coming in every day on the Railway Express . . . and I might add, going out that night. But LeGrande wound up locating twelve dogs.

"LeGrande picked up a good one in West Virginia named Willow Winds Mike, so that's what he named his kennels: Willow Winds. About that time Ned read an article by the noted gun dog writer of the day, Horace Lytle [a former *Field & Stream* gun dog editor], who was interested in crossbreeding.

"Now Lytle had a dog named Isley's Chip, an English setter, who had some of that old Campbell breeding in him. He was the son of the last setter at that time to have won the National Bird Dog Championship: Mississippi Zev.

"Later, Ned heard of a good bitch with a pro trainer down in South Carolina, and he went to see it. . . . Ned later said he paid an awful price for her. She was five years old, and he took her back to Pennsylvania. When he bred her to those cross-breeds that were all around, the breed was on the way again. She was Askew's Carolina Lady, she had nine litters, and she is recognized today as the foundation dam of the red setters. Almost every red setter running today goes back to her.

"Now Baynard and Church were also active. Church had bred up the Sunburst red setters. And Baynard was putting dogs around, and he sent one to a Marine flyer, Col. Ed Schnettler, who coincidentally had some red setters in Minnesota that went back to the old market gunner's dogs. Those old-timers wanted the red setter because it was tough in the wintertime, it took the cold water, and it would hop through the snow and everything.

"Schnettler developed a line that is still going today, the Saturday Night kennels. He developed a real producing sire in Saturday Night Ed in the late 1960s, which was used throughout the breed quite a bit.

"Then two men, Ernest Lewis of California and David Hasinger of Pennsylvania, came into it, and Hasinger had a pup he brought from

The late and immortal Buddwing with handler Don Beauchamp at their Kansas farm.

LeGrande Valley High Country, and he leased this dog to Lewis out in California. Well Lewis developed a line of red setters called the County Clare line, because his grandfather had come from County Clare in Ireland.

"By that time the red setter breed was getting pretty well established, and now I think we're far enough along to get the dogs qualified to run in the National Bird Dog Championship. The biggest all-breed, Field Dog Stud Book win to date was Paul Ober's [of Reading, Pennsylvania] championship at the New England Open All Age. That dog was named Celtic Sua Sponte. Paul's a lawyer and gives all his dogs legal names.

"Now the big names today are Don Beauchamp, a geologist, of Cheney, Kansas, and Roger Boser, a veterinarian of Seven Valleys, Pennsylvania. Boser presently has two dogs: Bearcat and Desperado, who were number one and two in the dog-of-the-year awards last year. Beauchamp has Motion Magic, a real contender. And oh yes, there's Bob and Katherine Gove of Princeton, Minnesota, who've got a great line of red setters."

BUDDWING

Bob stops to pet a mahogany-red head laying softly on his lap, and I ask him who's been the greatest red setter to date. He immediately names Buddwing, owned by Don Beauchamp. Buddwing had seventy Field Dog Stud Book wins when he died. (Buddwing was a favorite of mine. He won trials but he was also a character. I wrote a story about him in the book, *A Treasury of Happy Tails*.)

So what's the bottom line to all this?

THE CROSSBREEDING

Sprouse tells me, "The Field Dog Stud Book permitted the first crossbreeding of an English setter and a red setter in 1953, to create the new red setter. This was a milestone movement, for no other kennel club will permit crossbreeding. Ned LeGrande and Horace Lytle registered the first litter out of LeGrande's red setter dam Willow Wind's Smada, and Lytle's English setter sire, Isley's Chip.

"Now these were notable dogs. Smada Byrd was one of the great red setter field trial winners in the '20s. Smada became a powerful red setter line. And Isley's Chip, you'll remember, was the son of Mississippi Zev, the last English setter to win the National Bird Dog Championship.

"Even though more than half our members are bird hunters," says Sprouse, "our red setter roster also includes some field trial contenders who may qualify for the National Bird Dog Championship." There's a hint of a smile when he says, "Won't that be the day."

SO WHAT?

Yep, you learned no new training tips with Sprouse. So why did I tell the story? Two reasons.

I remember one night I was coon hunting with two chemical plant workers in mid-America. Somehow for some reason, one of them began bad-mouthing the wealthy, putting them down, saying they just got a leg-up with the judges.

I stopped the hunt to point out, "Is that right? Then tell me, where do you think the great dogs came from? England mostly," I answered. "And did they swim over here? Hardly. They were bought and paid for and imported—sometimes along with their handler.

"If it weren't for the rich, we'd have a mighty mediocre lot of dogs in this country today. All the good ones owe their existence on these shores to some Mr. Moneyfeller who paid not for a dog, but for a foundation sire or dam for all of us."

NO BOB'S NOT RICH

Bob rich? Maybe. I don't know. He lives in a two-room cabin in the sticks with his gang of red setters. I know he's tough and independent. If he needed medical care back in there they'd have to come drag him out with an Indian pony and travois—or a helicopter.

The reason I wanted you to know Bob is he's dedicated. He's spent his life building up a breed of gun dog. He couldn't walk; he had to sit; so he sat and worked with pen and paper and ended up making an equal contribution to anybody who ever went to field with a bird dog.

And you'll recall what I said about breeding. It makes up 95 percent of the dog, remember? And Bob's story points out breeding is not as simple and fortuitous as a cat finding a bird's nest on the ground. It takes many people, many generations, with many failures, to create a great gun dog line.

Roading red setter seems to pull truck through kennel gate.

SOMETHING ELSE

Later in this book you're going to read about a bird dog pro named Buddy Smith. He's a winner. And he's also a friend of Wilson Dunn, Grand Junction, Tennessee, owner of Dunn's Fearless Bud, an English pointer that won the National Bird Dog Championship in 1990.

Now Wilson likes Bob Sprouse. And Buddy Smith recently had a red setter from Bob in training. Well, Buddy also trains some pups for Wilson.

Oh yes, do you know this? It's very important. There's not a trainer in this book who is not an excellent puppy trainer. You know how few good puppy trainers there are? Most of the pros want a "made" dog they can go and enhance their reputation with.

You know the unique characteristics puppy trainers possess? We'll find out.

A DAY AFIELD

So get this. Buddy and Wilson gathered up this pup and carried him to Bob Sprouse's remote place and then wheeled the sportsman out onto the knoll of a hill. Wilson lingered and talked to Bob while Buddy walked far below to work Sprouse's pup in a clearing.

So what does this mean?

I don't care if you ain't got a nickel, or can't walk, or can't read, or see, or hear, or lift an arm. You can own a dog. And when you own a dog you don't own him alone. You enter into the fraternity of dogmen, which is the doggonedest fraternity I've ever found.

I'm talking about men who wouldn't give you the time of day if you met them on the street. But meet them in the field and you are immediately their equal, and you're someone to know, and someone to enjoy being with.

I've walked with Princes, shot rabbits for the Queen's corgies at Balmoral, hunted pheasant in France with a French governor and an army general, hunted rabbits with a small-town handyman, spent the weekend with a trustee released from prison that day so he could train a man's bird dogs, and flown in a private jet to waterfowl with an executive belonging to an exclusive duck club. I've gone afield with a fry cook, filling station attendant, share cropper, parson, undersecretary of the Interior (he backed over my tackle box filled with hunting accessories), Native American chief, civil rights activist, and on and on.

I've been with rowdies, incompetents, the mentally crippled, and street fighters.

I've called point for the scruffy and the elite, for the cordial and the hostile, for the town drunk and the bishop.

And on the day that I was with each of these men, they were the noblest, finest, friendliest, most cordial people I've ever known.

That's the real thing you get with a gun dog. You get respectability, acceptability, and the internal drive to spend a day without being an ass. For only good people have bird dogs.

Don't ever forget to thank the Sprouses of this world. They did an awful lot for you.

National field trial judge Bob Bullard and brace of English springer spaniels.

6

Bob Bullard

Field trials, especially those for retrievers, are under attack today for two reasons. 1) They don't resemble a day's hunt afield as their charter says they must, and 2) their ridiculous tests sometimes require dogs to trip over their God-given instincts in order to pass. If the dog can't or won't, he is too often brutalized into compliance.

I'm all for English springer spaniel (ESS) field trials. They do duplicate a day's hunt afield and therefore permit the gun dog trainer to use only sensible and humane training techniques. This especially includes tons of training birds. And that's the ideal.

Bearing all that in mind there are many essentials in developing any class hunting dog. But let's consider three. First, you must bond with the dog, so he's trained with love. This way a scowl on your face will prompt the dog to performance more than the whip in the hands of a nonthinker.

To bond with Pup you must bring him into your family life: the ideal being your home. But if this is not possible, then the hunting dog must be brought into as much nontraining contact with you as possible. Let him ride in the front seat to the store, walk on a leash around the block, frolic in the park with a ball, lay beside you as you read this book.

Second in our trilogy would be the need to train more than one class of gun dog, so we're enriched by the crossover.

And third, we must take our field trial campaigners out hunting. Heretofore many gun dog trainers assumed this would destroy Pup. They assumed it would make him loose on game and minimize some of the handler's control. But as we'll see here, the opposite is true.

Let's call up one case history to prove our point, then we'll discuss the personality to be showcased in this chapter.

Mike Flannery of Denver, Colorado, owned, trained, and handled River Oaks Corky. Corky became the first Lab to ever garner more than five hundred combined amateur and open field trial points. (Dale Lunsford of Spirit Lake, Iowa, and I were the co-judges who put this 500th point on Corky. At that time this was the highest total of field trial points ever achieved by a retriever.)

Contrary to the practice of that day, each of the three times Corky won the national Canadian championship, Mike hunted this champion on geese between field trial tests. So much for the experts saying a field trial dog can't be hunted. (Should you want to read about Corky see *Field & Stream*, March 1978.)

Now west of Portland, Oregon, in a small town called Cornelius, is an expert and compassionate veterinarian, gun dog trainer, field trial contender, national English springer spaniel championship judge, dust-grimed hunter, bona fide family man, farm hand, horse trainer, and all-around gun dog expert named Dr. Bob Bullard.

Bob's at the top of his game, at the peak of his life, and a keeper of all our faiths. He trains with love; he lives with his dogs; he hunts his field trial champions; yet he excels at the field trial game.

SEVEN-DAY HUNTS

Let's join Doc now in eastern Oregon, where he commonly hunts seven-day stretches and demands that dogs have lots of bottom in them.

In this old world there are three types of men. Those who talk about people, those who talk about things, and those who talk about ideas. Doc, who is mid-lifed, mid-height, and mid-weight, with soft hair and a perpetual smile, says out of nowhere as we cross a training field, "Food, water, and shelter. Or said another way: hunting, fishing, gardening, and shelter. These are man's basic instincts. Think of all those people who remodel their homes. I think of hunting in a very similar way as some do gardening. We re-enact our instincts today by hunting and fishing for food, planting a tomato, building a house. It's in our blood, our psyche, our very being."

Yes, Doc is a philosopher.

Five-time National Champion River Oaks Corky hands pheasant to Mike Flannery on his last hunt. Corky hunted till his dying day.

QUIET

He then tells me, "If cleanliness is next to godliness in some of our pursuits, I think in spanieling and bird hunting, quietness is next to godliness.

"I do a lot of hunting for these wild, woolly pheasants. And I'm not the world's best shot, I don't have the world's best dogs, but I'm a fair shot and I have good dogs. And I consistently do better than most other people. And there are three reasons for it.

"One is I'm out there all day; I'm pretty persistent. And I think I know how to hunt the territory. The other thing is I'm quiet.

"I remember one of the best mornings of my life, the best dog performance in my life, since real memorable dog performances are usually found in hunting situations and not in some field trial. Anyway, we were out in a good roosting area for these pheasants, and it was opening weekend, and there were several of us who were hunting this ranch. And we said, 'Well let's go out and post around some cattails and some weeds at the end of this pasture.'"

Doc whistles a dog down and casts him in another direction as he says, "We'd scouted this field before, and the dogs had shown us there were birds in there. But these guys—you know what they said that next morning? They said, 'Well we don't want any dogs in there while we're hunting. Cause we want it quiet.'"

THEY KNEW I HAD A GOOD DOG

"But a couple of guys in the group knew I had a good dog in Saighton's Storm [we visited the Welsh kennel of Saighton in *Field & Stream*, March 1975]. So it was finally agreed I could take Storm along. We posted two guns at the end of the beat [they were the blockers]. And the two guys who walked with me had never seen my dogs work.

"Well we all got there and waited for sunup, and I cast Storm off, and I never tooted a whistle. He made a cut to the left and a cast to the right, and he looked back at me, and I gave him a hand signal, and he made a figure 8, and I cast him off to the left, and boom! up goes a rooster.

"The two guys with me shoot the rooster, and it falls over in the cattails. And when they shoot, another rooster gets up, and they shoot him. All the time, mind you, there's been no whistle, no nothing. Just quiet. Then I motion for Storm to fetch. And Storm goes over and scoops it up."

DON'T PUSH THE BIRDS TOGETHER

"And while he's doing this one of the guys complains, 'Don't push the birds together or we'll lose our shooting.'

"I told him, 'Just wait.'

"After we made a nice double retrieve, we went on and worked the rest of that field. The birds were coming up every which way, and there was all kinds of shooting . . . and things did get noisy after that.

"But what I want to emphasize here is it was quiet. And if the average person had gone in there and yelled at his dog, crying 'Hup, Get Over, Hey, Watch it,' and all that stuff the noise would have lifted the whole field."

FABULOUS DOG PERFORMANCE

"Afterwards each of the hunters came up and said that was the most fabulous dog performance they ever saw. And I don't care if they said it or

Bob Bullard, far left, courses bird field with field trial springer before him.

not, it was a fabulous dog performance. And until somebody has experienced that, and until somebody has experienced hunting over a steady dog—which most people haven't—then thereafter they'll never again hunt with anything but a trained dog."

Doc thinks for a moment then offers, "Speaking of training, as a veterinarian I have to be a trainer all the time. You know, to teach people how to get along with their pets. How to *communicate*.

"I tell my clients dogs are like kids. Inasmuch as most of them will live up to your expectations. But if you expect this dog to sit on an examining table and be self confident, and not run from fear, nor shy away, then put him on the table, expect that of him, don't rush to him when he starts to jump off, and you know by the end of the examination that puppy is sitting there with self confidence. It does no good to have him sit there if we've put his tail between his legs. So I'm always training both dogs and people."

I've said this many times because I believe this manyfold. It's like the professor in the musical, Music Man. Remember?

He didn't know a note and conned the town into buying musical instruments from him so he could form the kids into a playing band.

When the instruments hit town it was his practice to draw his money and skidaddle. But alas, he'd fallen in love.

So he stayed and the day came for the parade and not a kid could toot a note. Well the professor told his charges, "To think the music and blow." He got away with it and, of course, won the girl.

So Doc Bullard is right. What you expect of a dog, and what you mentally transmit to a dog, will determine his behavior. Most people don't know this, but it's true.

WHAT YOU GET FROM HUNTING YOUR CHAMPION

Wanting to learn more about taking field trial champions hunting I ask Bob, "List some of the benefits of regularly hunting your campaign dogs."

He immediately starts, saying, "Birdiness. Hunting makes them birdy. Makes them inquisitive and aggressive. Then when I go to a trial, the dogs know what they're there for: to hunt birds. It's never in their mind to finish some test.

"Plus the hunting field trial champion learns how to handle terrain and cover. Nothing surprises him when he's competing because he's already grown comfortable in it, grown familiar with it.

"Hunting also relieves the tension. Not only in the pheasant field but at the trial. We've now bonded, we know each other, we've experienced all sorts of hunting situations together. So the dog runs more steadily at a trial; he uses his head more; he doesn't come unraveled when he meets the unexpected.

"For most handlers if they just compete in trials, the dog is always sensing their apprehension. And a nervous or confused dog can't hold true to his game. But for my champs . . . it's just another hunt. Only this time there's lots of people standing around with pencils and judges' sheets.

"No you can't beat hunting your field trial dogs," concludes Doc.

I ask, "Would you then recommend this for all field trial people?"

"Oh ho," he laughs, "some of them are die-hards. And others among them want silver . . . not dinner. No, let each handler decide for himself. But a hunter's what I am. If I had to choose between the two, the trial would be discarded. If others feel like that, then by all means, they're already hunting their champions."

Successful springer delivers to hand.

If you are campaigning a gun dog don't let the traditionalists talk you out of taking Pup to field. He'll love you for it, and you'll suddenly realize field trials are just games—but hunting is what it's all about.

REMEMBER MIKE GOULD

Now let's recall what Mike Gould was talking about in our first chapter. He said, "There is a dog above the field trial champion. And that's the hunting dog." Recall, too, all the things Mike listed the hunting dog must know and do that the field trial champion never confronts.

So handlers, like Dr. Bob Bullard, who can excel both at the hunt and at the game are truly extraordinary. Plus, they have dogs above the field trial champions. And they have dogs above the shooting dogs, too. They have the ultimate.

Only a few people achieve this. But those who do think the same way Doc does. He said, "If I had to choose between the two, I'd drop the trials."

How sweet it is.

Gary Ruppel with his hunting pointer watches TV at home. (Photo by Don Tolson)

7

Gary Ruppel

Gary should have been a priest. He is that kind, that concerned, that sooth-ing. And like St. Francis, Gary took his ministry to the animals. In both cases, the dogs were blessed.

How'd that song go? "What the world needs now is love, sweet love." Well that's become the ultimate truth in gun dog training.

For now we're with Gary Ruppel of Parker, Colorado, one of the new breed of professional gun dog trainers. I've come to ask this thirty-eight-year-old, slim-built, brown-haired, soft-mannered trainer, "How do you love-train a client's gun dog?"

Gary speaks softly, with joy, saying, "When I get the pups or dogs—especially a condo dog—I spend the first two or three days in the kennel with them. And I take them out and fun-walk them around the bird pens, down to the pond. I just really develop a good rapport with them. And I go into each kennel run every day to scoop, and I actually sit down on the concrete and tell them to come over. I tell them, 'Hey pardner, I'm okay.'

DOGS OUT OF STIR

"You know when you get some of these dogs in they're real spoiled and act like they've been put in a detention center. So I really try to develop that loving bond the first few days. Especially if I'm going to force-break them to do any kind of formal stuff. If there's going to be any kind of pressure I want to let them know I'm their buddy."

Gary also represents the new breed of gun dog trainer in training all breeds of gun dogs and advancing his theories and techniques through the richness of crossover training. He tells the client who brings him a Lab, "I'll make you a pointer out of him, or a traditional flushing dog. You tell me what you want."

THE WHOA POST

For any breed of dog the owner wants to point game, Gary first takes them to the training table. He says, "I start whoa-breaking them up there and then taking them to the whoa post." Okay, let's describe what Gary's talking about. A whoa table is belt high, some eight feet long, three feet wide with an over-passing wire cable to which the dog's collar is snapped.

The whoa post is a post buried in the ground with a check cord attached to Pup's collar. The trainer has another check cord attached to a second collar that's toward the front of Pup's neck with which he coaxes the dog to walk forward upon the command to heel. Just before the whoa-post cord tightens to pull the whoa-post collar, the trainer says, "Whoa." Now back to Gary.

"The first week on the table I just put them up there and brush them, and give them cookies, and love them. I've got a bad back, so I don't want to lift those big dogs, and I require them to jump up there. Which means I've got to make the tabletop attractive or they'll tell me, 'No way.'

"Consequently I make the tabletop a fun place to go, and they do jump up there for training.

"Now if I'm teaching whoa, say to a Lab, I get them up on the table and tell them whoa. If they move, I pick them up and put them back where they left, saying whoa, whoa. They learn real fast. And that's because they hate to be picked up. That's right, if they move I physically pick them up, take away their four feet, and put them on the spot they vacated [Think about it. Human, horse, or dog, take away their feet, and they're yours.] Then later I put a check cord on them and direct them back and forth across the table, getting them to go with the lead.

"And then I go to the whoa post and from that to the field. After I whoa-break them, I introduce them to the birds again. When they enter the planted bird's scent cone I say, whoa. And I have taught whoa real strong on the table and in the field, so I don't have to go to the dog and physically hold him before birds.

Making sure no one's gun-shy, Gary works gun and bird in front of chain gang. (Photo by Don Tolson)

"But there is never a bird shown on the table. I don't want these beginning dogs to associate any negative training with birds.

INTRODUCING THE BIRD

"Now all beginning dogs go through a flattening-out process. You know, head down, tail down, ears down. No dog likes to stop on whoa . . . they want to go, go, go. But after a while they start to pump up. So after they are really pumped up, that's when I introduce the bird.

"I plant the bird and have a bird boy flush it after the Lab has established point. Or any breed of dog for that matter. At first it's real low-keyed. I just want to be successful. But later I make a big deal out of it. A lot of hurrahing and letting the bird boy wave the bird around and entice the dog.

REQUIRING THE OWNER GET INVOLVED

"In everything I do, I put the ultimate dog performance on the shoulders of the owner. I get them involved, which many pros don't do. That way I can go home at night and feel good about the dog and myself.

"You know," Gary continues, "some of the trainers say, 'This is what I did to the dog; take him, and good luck.' That's worthless. Get the owner out training, let him learn exactly what you're doing, and why. And I will admit, it's a lot harder to train the owner than it is his dog."

Practically every trainer featured in this book requires the owner learns how to train his dog, learns to handle his dog, and learns what the pro is doing and why he's doing it.

Also, if these trainers are breeding and placing pups with the hunting public, they screen the human prospects. That's right. Their emphasis is not the person picking a pup from the litter. It's the trainer picking the right person from the mass who come to see their pups.

Later you'll meet a Sacramento trainer specializing in flat-coat retrievers who will absolutely not sell a pup to a hunter who intends to use a shock collar in training. His reasoning? It's so easy to train a dog with love, why torture it and end up with nothing.

And finally, these trainers all try to make the dog feel like he's their one and only. It's no longer an impersonal relationship between trainer and pupil. Note that Gary tells us he's handing out cookies.

I spend as much time as I can with Gary—and we talk a lot about dogs. One time he told me, "I can't stand for someone not to like me. Same with a dog. That dog comes into my kennel, and he's looking at me with a scowl—you can tell!—a real scowl, and that scowl is saying, 'You're a jerk,' or something like that.

"I can't stand it. So I'm down on my knees loving that guy, telling him I'm actually all right. Trying to dispel any bad notions he has of me. Trying to confirm with all his senses that everything is going to be all right."

And that's the new breed of gun dog trainer.

Far cry from the old days. And hallelujah.

THE JOY OF FOUR-WEEK-OLD PUPS

I like Gary: he's always smiling and always thinking good, and he has fun

Gary brings water to chain gang. (Photo by Don Tolson)

Crossover training makes a trainer. Here Gary handles a German shorthair, an English setter, a Brittany, and several Labs. (Photo by Don Tolson)

with life. He says, "I get these one-year-old dogs out of some Denver condominium. They've never seen a bird in their life. That's the challenge. But, nevertheless, they are trainable.

"But what I really like is a litter of four-week-old pups. Say it's 95 degrees, so I take them all to the pond. And I put pigeons in their kennel run and let them fuss with them. I do that everyday. And when they are six weeks old, I'll take the bitch and the whole litter down to the pond and throw two dummies out there. One for the bitch and one for the puppies. They jump right in, they are competitive, and they want to stay with their brothers and sisters. Pointers or retrievers, I do the same thing."

BONDING

"Now you've got to bond with a dog before you can train him. And you may be surprised to learn the best way to bond is through obedience training. But if it's a dog that really likes people and likes to be around me, say eight months old, then I'll give them birds at first. Let them chase, you know. Pump them up on birds, then go to obedience."

I say to Gary, "You were using the old-time training methods when you started training. Now you've mellowed to this intimacy thing. What did you see as the result of the two approaches?"

Gary shows his pleasure with it all when he answers, "Dogs are part of our families now, and our best friends. And one of the reasons I was able to develop this bonded training is *I got into a better line of dogs. The Labs that I have now are much more sensitive than they used to be, and if you trained like we did in the old days, you wouldn't get the response that you do now with the love and tenderness. These dogs can't take that old-time pressure because they are a lot more intelligent than the Lab string used to be. Good selective breeding has made good, sensitive Labs."* Remember this. This paragraph may be the most important in the book.

BREEDING

And to that end we'll meet a breeder who has accomplished this very thing. It's even said his dogs come from the womb congenitally trained. What's meant by that is the dogs are so amenable to training. They are eager and pliable pupils.

Gary Ruppel and Mike Gould train a lot together. Here Gary follows with brace pointers to honor while Mike walks dog into bird's scent cone.

Gary's saying, *"These dogs are born trained. What I mean by that is their sensitivity makes them adaptable to a very soft process of training. Instead of problem dogs now, we are getting problem-solving dogs—"*

I interrupt, "That's the great thing that's happened this century with our gun dogs." I'm so pleased with this trainer: he's bright, conscientious, mellow, and most importantly—successful.

THE WHISTLE-TRAINED DOG

He continues, "You get so many more results from the dog at the end now, and so much more respect. It's phenomenal. Here, let me get this five-month-old pointer out of the truck. I took her out when she was a baby, and I developed all her natural instincts, and now, at five months, she'll go out and point every time and retrieve to hand. All because of the bonding we have. *She was developed with fun-association and bird-association.* All with the whistle when she was a baby."

WHISTLE WHILE YOU TRAIN

"Here's how it's done. *Every time I whistle . . . something good is going to happen to the dog.* Something positive. Whether it's food or a treat or a pat on the head or birds. Of course that's her favorite thing: birds. All puppies have bird exposure when they are four weeks old. Plus, I'm whistling the whole time to establish the fun-association . . . and when we get her out in a minute she'll come, and when I put the bird out there, she'll retrieve it to hand. And that's all because she loves me, and she wants to please me."

Well folks that's what we're seeing all over America. The new breed of gun dog trainers and their love-trained dogs. Intimidation in training is out, intimacy in training is in. Like the song says, it's "love, sweet love," and how happy I am it's all come about.

As setter delivers to hand, Bill Moore rears him up for a loving. That's bonding.

8

Bill Moore

In the old days there were good things to be had and good things to be said about field trials. Since then, and too often, field trials foster dogs that can't or don't hunt for the gun, and some trainers who in order to win at all costs resort to brutality. Meet Bill Moore who revived all the good things about field trials by winning the national championship with a borrowed dog trainer, a borrowed shotgun, and a dog who lived in a fifty-five-gallon barrel.

Bill Moore was just a good ol' country boy who worked at the McNairy Farmer's Co-op in Selmer, Tennessee, was interested in English setters, and hunted bobwhite on weekends.

If Bill had been content to do just that and be just that, we'd never have heard of him. But that could never be after a bunch of dogs came along named Tricky Dick.

Bill tells us, "A man named Bill Davis had a little female setter called Pinnacle's Cricket they were training, and she got into a fence and broke a hip. Well he gave her to me, and I fixed her hip back up and bred her to Tomaka's Tricky Dick at Randy Downs down here.

"She had three male puppies: Tennessee Tricky Dick and Tricky Dick Jim, and another one I sold young.

"At a year old we started running these two setters in this new competition called National Shoot To Retrieve Association (NSTRA) where a foot hunter can handle his dog through a bird field, and if everything goes right, he can make a champion.

THE CHAMPIONS

"Well I started placing at a year old, and at two year's old, both dogs were champions. Then in '84 I won the NSTRA Champion of Champions [one of four national events held each year] with Tennessee Tricky Dick. And then I got him run over and killed Thanksgiving Day while I was bird hunting. [This is important: hunting a national champion. Bill knew it was the best thing he could do for the dog.]

"We had sold Tricky Dick Jim, so I went back and bought him, and then I went and bought another dog I called Tricky Dick at three months old. And then the Jim dog first won the NSTRA Dog of the Year [the daddy of all NSTRA trials] in '87. Then in '88 I won the Champion of Champions, and then in '89 I won all four of the major trials with Dick and Jim.

"Now in eleven years runnin' I won eleven of the major championships. Got eleven firsts, a second, and a third with these three or four dogs . . . but most of it's been done with two dogs. I have won more than any man ever won in shoot to retrieve."

Listening to Moore I realize it's like they say down here, "That's not braggin', that's fact." I look at the forty-nine-year-old, five-foot-ten-inch, 170-pound, blue-eyed, twangy-speakin' training-wonder and ask myself why dame fortune shined on him. But it's that way with people who train dogs. Most of the great dog people were made by one dog: Bill Moore was made by three.

WHAT MAKES A CHAMPION?

I ask him, "What do you look for in a dog—it's evident you pick the winners."

Moore says, "I look for a lot of speed and intelligence; I want a smart dog that's natural. [This "smartness" will come up time and again in this book as the determinant in picking a pup.]

"I want," continues Moore, "to get a natural dog you don't have to do a lot of things to. [Remember in the introduction I told you we wanted a God-made dog, not a human-made dog for breeding. We want a dyed-through dog, not something just human-dipped and colored on the surface.]

"And," adds Moore, "you want a personal dog that's got a lot of sense and wants to please you. It's a lot easier to train him than one of those old hardheads.

"I want a dog that likes to go, because I work my dogs a good bit. I start that puppy out and get him into liking his birds, you know, and keep repeating and pet him a lot. I don't believe in beating 'em."

LOTS OF BIRDS

"Gotta give lots of birds. After you get these dogs working birds you shoot birds over them three or four days a week at home and go to trials on weekends.

"Conditioning is a big factor. If you don't get your dog in good condition, there's no need going nowadays. You got to have a dog . . . like an old fellow told me, 'There's a line you know. One side of the line is a renegade. The other side of the line is a over-broke dog. You've got to keep him on that line.' So that's what I do shootin' birds all week.

"Because I noticed that ol' man was right. These dogs—you get them doing good, and you get them over here, and you have to do something to get them back. You got to watch them everyday. And this dog does one thing, and this dog does another thing. Like right now I got one running and not hunting. And you've got to get him from running and back to hunting. But you got to let him run, too. So you've got to figure out what to do.

"But if anybody wants a bird dog, they gonna haf' to get him into lots of birds, they're gonna haf' to hunt him. They can't do it once a week. They got to get out there and work the dog.

"Now you get a good ol' broke dog that's got some age on him, you can do it. But you get a puppy—and most people wants to buy a puppy who have never worked a bird dog—and become a first-time trainer. And that don't work."

PUPPIES FOR SALE

"I get so many calls for puppies. I'm at that phone all night. And I tell 'em what I breed is a walking, foot-shooting dog. As far as saying my dogs are going to run all-age, I don't care. We've got dogs doing that, and my dogs are capable. But it's a different world. You've got to train different for field trials, but these dogs will run with anybody's dogs.

"They're a snappy-running dog, yet they've got enough sense to come and foot-hunt with you, and you can put them where you want them.

"I carry my dogs wild-bird hunting today. I field trial them tomorrow, and the next day I go back to wild-bird hunting. The only thing he'll do, if you wild-bird him while you're trialing is he'll work his scent easier. What I mean [is] he'll gait himself bird hunting. Where in these trials, they run as wide and hard as they can. But you go to wild-bird hunting this dog, and he'll gait himself and be slower. Now some dogs go over the line. When that happens, just stand him up two weeks, and when you let him out, don't bird hunt him, and just run him in trials, and he'll go back to normal. Dogs are adaptable. They're bright."

PEN-RAISED BIRDS

"Now folks tell me you take a dog on tame birds, and he'll run up wild birds. Well that's crazy. They say a dog can't change . . . he'll get so close to the wild ones he'll bump 'em up. That's crap. I can run mine all spring and fall on liberated birds, and I carry him out wild-bird hunting the first day, and he'll point 'em from here to the road."

"Well Bill," I tell him, "that's all very good, but you've yet to tell me why some other man wasn't the winningest handler instead of you. You had to have done something different."

THE BOND

Bill Moore's not one to dally, so he jumps right on it, saying, "I contribute my winning to having good, smart dogs that's got some sense and some willpower and wants to run. Then you've got to have that dog that's on the same wavelength as you. He's got to know what you're wanting, and you've got to know what he's wanting. You all get to be where you can both read each other's minds.

"That's what I think has been really good on my dogs. People say, 'Why those dogs just know what you're thinking. And you know what they're thinking.' And that's what you got to have. You've got to have that bond.

"At NSTRA trials, that dog's got to know what to do without your

Not only can Tricky setters win national championships and then take you bird hunting, they also look good doing it.

talking to him. You use a lot of hollering and calling, and they'll cut your obedience down. You see, we get scored on find, retrieve, ground coverage, back, and obedience. And at the end of each brace they score on each of these things and put the score on a board for everyone to see. At the end of the day the guy with the highest numbers wins the trial.

"To make an NSTRA champion you've got to have eighteen points. Nine of them got to be first place. At a local trial, you get three points for first, two for second, and one for third."

THE OLD CLASSIC CIRCUIT

I ask Moore, "Before NSTRA all we had in this country was the big, classic field-trial, bird-dog circuit. What would you have done in those days?"

He says fast, "I couldn't have afforded to run. What I like about shoot-to-retrieve is you can take the poorest, lowest man on the pole, and I've got as good a chance to win as this millionaire that's sitting over there in that Cadillac. We turn loose in that field, and I've got the same brace he's got, he can't buy the judges, and there is no politics in our trial."

"How did you get away from politics?"

He answers, "You see you got two judges, and they switch halfway through the brace. So both judges judge both dogs.

"And you got your score on the board. So no judge can change his mind, and it's for sure nobody can change that score. What you get is what you got.

"I beat pros; I beat millionaires," says Moore. "When I go up there and turn that dog loose, I got the same shot as everybody else has."

TALK ABOUT HARD TIMES

"I'll never forget when my wife and I went up to my first national in Indiana. *I dug ol' Tennessee Tricky Dick out of a fifty-five-gallon barrel that was his house, borrowed a dog wagon from Garry Shurratt, borrowed a shotgun from Ricky Roten, went up there blind, didn't know nobody. Tom Burks got me a room at a motel and showed me how to hunt the grounds. . . . He was the first president of NSTRA. And I won the thing. I won the national.* And now I won eleven of 'em. It's a good world that NSTRA."

And I'm thinking, "It's a good family of dogs those Tricky Dicks." And I'm thinking, too, it's a good country we have in the USA. When greed and ego and politics and money are kicked in the butt and kept away from your dog life.

Bill Moore kicked it. Bill Moore won.

You can, too.

WHAT MOORE SAID

It's deceptive. The words come so easy and simple. But Bill Moore taught us a lot in this short visit. He said he demanded smart dogs that had good breeding and the greatness was born in them, not plastered on.

He said birds make a dog. Lots of birds.

He said any field trial champion worth his salt will adjust his range for a foot hunt and do an excellent job of it.

He said I get a puppy into lots of bird and love him a lot. Remember? And he said the man and dog have got to bond. Isn't that what this book is about?

He said you can't train a dog one day a week, you've got to train him every day. And that's what I call commitment. Commitment to me is time and concern and thinking ahead and always doing the best you can for your dog.

Finally, he said—and I like this the best, "You and your dog have got to be able to read each other's minds."

Now folks, this ain't no put-on dude. Some guy with wing tips and a feather in his straw hat and a gardenia in his bib overalls. This is sure'nuf, down-home, no-nonsense, use-it-only-if-it-works Bill Moore, and if he says dogs can read your mind then it's fact.

If you still don't think so then tell me what time you're going to be at the McNairy Farmer's Co-op to take on Bill Moore. I want to be there.

Butch Goodwin and Maggie.

9

Butch Goodwin

Maybe of all the trainers, I'm most proud of Butch Goodwin. You see Butch endured the pain of conversion. He was the typical American button pusher thinking he could train dogs with impersonal, high-pressure, electric-collar rigidity and pain. Then after years of criticism by fellow dog trainers, and years of internalizing his dilemma, Butch one day converted to the standards presented in this book. Oh not all of them. But the electric shock collar is gone. And that's a success I wish could be duplicated by every pain-trainer in America today.

Pain, brutality, and barbarianism ain't dog training.

And a lot of Americans don't know that.

They've got their electric cattle prods, and their electric shock collars, and their BB-loaded whips, and their boot toes, and chains, and BB guns, and shotguns, and slingshots, and a whole arsenal of pain-inflicting weaponry, and they've been taught the way to train a dog is to make his life sheer hell.

They've especially been taught this if they follow the classic field-trial retriever circuit. Because many of the tests at those events are so artificial the dogs can't imagine them, and when they, therefore, fail the test, some trainers damn near kill the dog in the next training session so he'll be sure to pass the nonsense test the next time he sees it. It's the truth.

And Butch wanted to be a retriever field trial winner.

So in many ways Butch was training like most of the retriever trainers trained. And as many still do today.

Not that Butch was brutal. He wasn't and he ain't. Matter of fact, at six feet four inches, nearly three hundred pounds, I find him to be a pussycat. His true essence is kindness, care, concern, love, and compassion. So in truth, Butch was playing a game totally alien to his very core.

And he was playing this game in front of Mike Gould (chapter 1) and Gary Ruppel (chapter 7). That is, he was training with them everyday. Or else, he would be on the other side of the pasture, doing his thing. But he could still glance across the field and see Mike and Gary going about their motivation drills instead of resorting to electricity.

Earning a shout of "Will wonders never cease?" from me when Butch announced he was finished with the electric collar, he would, nevertheless, take no credit for his redemption. And he still maintains a dog must always be under control. They can't be brought along to run wild the way Mike and Gary say—and prove—they can.

So that makes for what follows. Listen to Butch Goodwin of New Plymouth, Idaho, Chesapeake Bay retriever training specialist. Listen to a man made good, to do good, with dogs.

A PRIVATE PRINTING PLANT

A while back, Butch bought a computer and took to it like a dog takes to chicken gravy. Clients, friends, critics, everyone started getting reams of paper defining what Butch Goodwin stood for and how he went about his training and his life. His computer publications finally ended up in color.

In other words, Butch ain't the tall, silent type. No, not hardly. Butch has lots to say and says it.

THE NEW BUTCH

First off, Butch tells us, "My biggest training gripe has always been the new retriever owner doesn't do his share in the early training, socializing, and bonding with a young dog."

Gary Ruppel also emphasizes this whenever he talks to you or anyone else. For example, he keeps asking me to write a puppy book and explain to new clients what they must do to contribute to the success and well-being of their shooting dogs. How the clients must visit the kennels often and gradually take over both the training and the handling of the new prospects.

Butch working Chesie pup on dummy drill.

Okay, back to Butch. He says, "Early training and socialization and bonding will make more difference in a dog's later life . . . than any other nongenetic factors. Early training and socialization are critical!"

Wow, I love that. Sure a far cry from a senseless shock collar trainer, heh what?

Butch says, "Pup must have exposure to environment factors which teach him to deal with adversity later. Bonding is the catalyst which allows Pup to trust and work in unity with the trainer. And, regardless of how well-bred Pup is, inadequate early training, socialization, and human bonding can override all of his outstanding genetic traits. Unfortunately, I see this lack of early training almost every day.

"If only the owner had taken the time to expose his pup to a greater variety of environmental situations and done some early training, I wouldn't have to take the time to coax him through a puppy problem. Instead, I'd be spending my time training him.

"Housebreaking may be the first form of real obedience that a pup will receive. Other than that, once he knows his name and understands the meaning of the word 'no,' and to come when called, I believe that a retriever pup should be started retrieving. These pre-obedience retrieving games are of utmost importance. Retrieving with a ball is a good way to start. (I like to use a racquetball rather than a tennis ball, as it is smaller and more difficult to destroy.)

"As the pup gets older I switch to bird wings and then gradually introduce dead birds and then live, clip-wing pigeons. I use pigeons with puppies because they are readily available, cheap, and relatively benign. Live ducks and pheasants can injure a pup and cause problems which will last a lifetime. I don't believe you can get a pup used to a real bird (dead or alive) early enough."

PRE-STRESSING

"I've been very successful 'pre-stressing' pups. I find the very young ones, exposed to every kind of surface, a variety of sounds, a variety of obstacles, and of course water, birds, and gunfire (while his attention is on something more important—such as food), learn that they can survive any adversity that comes their way.

"A pup must learn he really doesn't need help to be in control in nearly any situation. The pup that learns only to expect help will not be capable of coping on his own with life's stresses.

"This is very important to the early training of a gun dog pup as he must learn early on to think and cope for himself. He must learn this now because later on he will have to be able to think on his feet. And a pup that is able to think and cope for himself *grows into an adult dog which doesn't have to be dominated in order to get the best out of him in his future training.*"

DOMINATION IN GUN DOG TRAINING IS DEAD

What an excellent concept. You see, domination in gun dog training is dead. And here Butch shows us how to diminish it—or avoid it. Good thinking, Butch, you're getting more fun for me, and more valuable for the dogs everyday.

Butch then tells us, "When I get a new retriever into my kennel to train, I like to start by just walking with him around in the fields. I stop occasionally and sit down and just play with him. I'm amazed at the number of dogs that just can't loosen up—they can't play. Often I'll roll them on their backs and try to scratch their bellies. Perhaps they think it's a form of domination, but many of these newcomers are too uptight to allow me to show them any affection.

"I try not to get too involved in whatever it is they want to do and where they want to explore. I just want to observe how they handle every new environment with me, a stranger, who is trying to be nice to them.

"This tells me a lot about their willingness to cooperate, or their independence. Amazingly, many don't handle any of this very well. I feel that I learn a lot very quickly about how they are going to handle things when it comes time to turn the 'wanna' into the 'gotta.'"

GETTING PERSONAL

"Another thing I like to do early on is put a newcomer up on my force-fetch table and allow them time to get used to the table and then brush them, and examine them from head to toe. I open their mouths, pick up their feet, mess with their rears, run my hands under their belly. I spit in their mouths! Did I say spit in their mouths? Yuck—yea, but it works."

Later you'll be reading the profile of Ken Osborn, a flat-coat retriever specialist in Sacramento, California. Ken says the same thing. He spits on his fingers and "feeds" this to each pup. Also, Bob Wehle, a gun dog breeding specialist who you'll also meet later, has built a love table in front of his kennel runs. Each released dog runs to the table, leaps up, and stands there as Bob breathes in his face. It's probably the most effective way of bonding and maintaining the bond.

TEACHING THROUGH ABUSE

Butch then confides, "When I worked for a field trial trainer, I saw, almost every day, trainers come on board who knew nothing about how and why a dog does what he does. They believed the only way to train a dog was through abuse. They were just out to teach the SOB a lesson. I believe Bob Wehle [now Butch's referring to him] when you wrote, Bill, that he said, 'you train with the tone of your voice, your mannerisms, your expression. I believe a dog knows when you're smiling. Certainly they know the inflection in your voice.'"

"Within a day or so after a new dog arrives," Butch continues, "I like to begin basic obedience, but this formal training session is always followed up with a short, unrestricted run around the field."

Here's where Butch and Mike Gould and Gary Ruppel still disagree.

Chesie returns with dummy and asks, "Was that alright Boss?" (Photo by Tammy Norton)

The latter two want their pups unfettered, running wild, never hearing the word no. Butch says, "Not possible. You've got to have control of the dog if for no other reason than he could run off and get lost."

LEARNING TO LEARN

Now Butch explains, "A pup's learning is no different from a young child's. They have to start with kindergarten-type lessons and gradually build on a solid foundation until they reach a satisfactory level. All of the behavior lessons that a finished retriever is expected to perform are started at the trainer's side. If you don't have control of the dog at your side, you will never have control at a distance.

"Similarly, if you don't have a solid foundation of training and 'learning to learn,' everything which is built on that foundation will eventually crumble. You hear athletic coaches stress 'fundamentals' [Butch was a linebacker for the University of Arizona Wildcats] and probably get tired of hearing it, but training a dog is not different from coaching an athletic team—I can't overstress the need for solid basics, i.e., fundamentals.

"In order to pile the building blocks on top of one another in the correct sequence and to guarantee that at some point the structure doesn't crumble, I spend most of the first month training on obedience. This is obedience that is expected of any gun dog."

Now as delightful as all this is, Butch goes on page after page explaining his training philosophy and techniques. If you want to read the rest of what he has to say, write and ask him to send it (he will). Contact him at Northern Flight Retrievers, Butch Goodwin, 4965 Freemont Road, New Plymouth, Idaho, 83655.

And send some coins taped to cardboard to defray Butch's mailing costs.

HIS HOLY GRAIL

So I cut off Butch since I figure you now have the feel for what he's about. He wants humane training, and he wants up-front control.

But that's not Butch's Holy Grail in life. No, that's natural ability in gun dogs. So let's turn to that interest—that passion—of his.

Butch tells us, "Last fall I attended a NAVHDA [North American Versatile Hunting Dog Association—this is an organization that tests the continental breeds] natural ability test. This was very soon after I returned form the AKC Master National Hunt Test. I was, at that time, very disgruntled over the fiasco the AKC called the 'Master National.' This was supposed to be the showcase of the AKC hunt test program and instead it was a travesty. It had nothing to do with hunting. [What did I tell you? Not only doesn't the field trial circuit duplicate hunting tests, neither do the hunting retriever tests.] So my attending a NAVHDA test was to look at how this organization tests their pointing breeds.

"I was very impressed with what I saw [most everybody is]. It was truly a total testing and evaluation of versatile hunting dogs. It didn't matter how much money the owners had because year-round, professional training was unnecessary (each amateur can train his own dog). Also, politics seemed to be at a minimum, the dogs had to look like a representative of their breed was expected to look, the dogs had to allow a stranger to physically examine them, and then perform and demonstrate their *developed natural abilities* in a series of tests.

"The dogs were graded in a noncompetitive manner. Then all this information was recorded and computerized for all to see. A real bonus for anyone interested in breeding [is] to know the attributes that the dog under test, or the entire litter, was born with.

"It seemed like such a simple concept—why hadn't the retriever crowd been able to put together something like this in all of these years? Why? Could it be because the AKC is only interested in registration fees? Because they have no interest in the betterment of the breeds—just in the money that the dogs can generate?"

NATURAL ABILITY

"During the next week, I sat down with a NAVHDA judge (who, by the way, used to have Chesapeakes and ran field trials, and got fed up with the BS and switched to pointers, and attempted to develop an outline of traits necessary for natural ability testing in order to evaluate retrievers.")

INHERITABLE TRAITS

After managing that yard-long sentence, Butch then outlines his desire to develop a list of inherited natural abilities of retriever breeds, and a testing format.

Butch calls gang together to say, "You may wonder why I've called this meeting..." (Photo by Tammy Norton)

He posts the following:

"Nose: A dog without a good nose is all but worthless, scenting ability is far and away the most important of all the canine senses. Why [the] AKC eliminated the category of Nose from their judging criteria, I'll never understand.

"Search: Search is a combination of Nose and Desire. A retriever that knows only to sit at the handler's side and be under total control of the handler and is not expected to Search for lost birds, won't find many lost birds in a true hunting situation. I truly believe that Search is a developed natural ability that is of utmost importance.

"Tracking: This is another combination of Nose and Desire coupled with the instinct to Retrieve. Each of the retriever testing organizations talks about the ability to track a cripple, yet NAHRA is the only one that has a true Tracking test.

"Desire: A retriever gun dog without the inherited Desire to do his job is worthless. Some show ring retrievers are perfect examples. *I have seen trainers force dogs to do the job they should be doing instinctively. Genetically these dogs are worthless as breeding stock. Also, if a dog has to be forced to do his God-given job out of fear, he's worthless. Desire is the passport to greatness that reveals itself even in a youngster.*"

I believe what Butch is saying. I feel now—I didn't used to—but I feel now that 95 percent of everything good in a hunting dog is put there by God, while only 5 percent is plastered on by humans. I say it this way, too: You can't shoot 12-gauge shells out of a .22 rifle. In other words, you can't get more than you've got if it ain't there to begin with.

But now get this—this is important. The classic field trial circuit tests retrievers on nonhunting, nonsense tests. Consequently, the talent and genius the retriever was born with, in other words his natural ability to hunt and fetch, is atrophied by a testing format that wants to *see what the trainer put in*. Thus the domination and barbarianism that often accompanies field trial retrieverdom comes to pass.

Now back to Butch, as he says, "Retrieving is a direct function of Desire, and the two go hand-in-hand. Birdiness is an important example of natural Retrieving ability. Testing for the natural Retrieving instinct of future breeding stock should be of primary importance to the breeder. None of the retriever testing organizations has a test for natural Retrieving ability in young or untrained dogs. Each organization tests only the *trained* ability to retrieve by throwing marks.

"Chase: The inherent interest to Chase objects should be very strong in the retrieving breeds. I believe that a retrieving dog that shows little interest in the Chase is often not going to be very bold or very solid in his temperament.

"Fetch and Carry: The young retriever should show his desire and love of retrieving by picking up objects and carrying them around. With a minimum of development the retriever should exhibit his instinct to Fetch and Carry a variety of objects, especially birds and feathers.

"Hardmouth: I truly believe the predisposition for Hardmouth, like the predisposition for gun-shyness, can be passed on genetically. Perhaps it is due to a certain lack of willing cooperation. Perhaps it is a very strong desire to retrieve for food. Perhaps it is genetic independence. From the standpoint of a breed I think it is something that needs to be tested and evaluated at an early age. Hardmouth is something which is often masked with force-fetch. Personally I'm not sure that it is ever really curable, but I would rather not have the inclination in my breeding stock.

"Gun-shyness: I repeat, Gun-shyness is a genetic trait. Obviously, Gun-shyness can be a man-caused problem, and it is a problem which can be masked. But my concern is actually with the inherited nervous condition which produces a pup that shows any predisposition toward shyness.

"Love of water: If you go on the assumption—as I do—that the majority of retrievers used for hunting in the U.S. today are used primarily for waterfowl hunting, then it only makes sense that developing Love of water is necessary in a breeding program. I see dogs almost monthly that have tremendous fear of water. I have to teach them to swim. Perhaps much of this is the fault of their owners for not doing any early positive association with water. I like to see my young breeding prospects feel very comfortable in water. I truly believe the dog's feeling of comfort in water is a genetically inherited trait which only needs nurturing to develop an exceptional water retriever.

"Cooperation: I believe there are few traits which can influence the future development and training of any hunting prospect more than Cooperation. If you consider Cooperation to be directly related to the combination of Intelligence and Training, then it becomes immediately apparent that much of the future training and experience which produces a reliable retriever is influenced by these inherited traits.

"I watch future prospects for intelligence, willingness to please, and immediate grasp of early training. I also truly believe that the eyes give much of this away. A dog that won't look me in the eye is often trying to avoid cooperation. The one that can't take his eyes off me and intently watches my every move I consider to be very intelligent and trainable."

SELECTIVE BREEDING

Having finished his list of traits, Butch then says, "Bill, if we were able to evaluate and record these natural abilities, along with the prospect's physical attributes and genetically inherited diseases, we would have a program second to none for selectively breeding the finest, genetically sound,

Butch and two young buddies contemplate where to go from here. Won't matter as long as they're together. (Photo by Tammy Norton)

working retrievers that the hunter could possibly want.

"Now Mr. Wehle has proven time and time again—I got this from your article—that the breaking is in the breeding, not in the training. Then Mr. Wehle says he doesn't like to outcross because he doesn't know what's really in another kennel's dog or [what's] been glossed over by training.

"Wehle says, 'I've had a lot of dogs with genetically inherited characteristics that I had to correct or cover over with training. The problem is still in the blood, though, and I don't want them in my breeding program.' Hurray for Mr. Wehle. Too many breeders refuse to see beyond the title and the glitter. They'd never look at the whole dog and the attributes and deficiencies that he was born with!"

Well, Butch, we're mighty indebted to you. And mighty enlightened by you. You've come a long way, Pardner, and I now know there's no limit to how far you'll go in space-probe dog training and understanding.

Because that's what marks the new gun dog trainers. They think. Simple, isn't it? They study and experiment and think. Used to be the trainer just went through the exercises by rote. No more. Every unique thing a pro now sees in a dog calls for sitting down and ruminating over it. And coming up with a new technique to handle it.

There's so much that is fascinating in dog training now. And it's trainers like you, Butch, who are making the contributions.

Ken Osborn and flat-coat take time out on hunt to pause by old sickle bar. "What flat-coats make is hunters, not field trialers," says Osborn.

10

Ken Osborn

Ken Osborn is the rarest of all gun dog trainers. His specialty is flat-coat retrievers. Now folks, you ain't going to see a flat-coat retriever if you hang around gun dogs for ten years. They're that scarce. But that's not why Ken appears here. Hardly. Ken appears here because he's one of the new breed of nonstress gun dog trainers. And I discover he's a good one.

I've never met the guy. He wrote and said he trained the way I said you should. So I'm getting off this plane in Sacramento, California, looking for a tall man with sunken cheeks, bowed neck, hatchet shoulder blades—for that's the way St. Francis of Assisi, the friend of animals, is usually portrayed.

You've seen the same thing. The limp wrist, the watery eye, the shallow breathing.

But who steps up? A participant in World Championship Wrestling? Thick wrists, chalk eyes, granite chin, five feet eight inches, two hundred pounds. This man could rip a five-hundred-year-old sequoia from the earth. I can't grasp his hand fully when we shake. I envision him entering the ring wearing a whistle lanyard and toting a set of scoop tools. A raucous band would intone "You Ain't Nothin' But a Hound Dog." So much for expectations!

For here he is this sensitive trainer, this gentle trainer, and most important, this thinking trainer. For later Ken will show me his dog library. I'm in the dog business and his bookcase makes eight of mine.

So here's Ken Osborn. Enjoy!

THE FLAT-COAT RETRIEVER

Ken's been in the dog business all his adult life. He went through all that field trial thing, but now trains only gun dogs.

Of course he'll take any bona fide sporting dog to train (I counted about twenty Brittanies), but his love is the flat-coat retriever.

This rare dog looks like a thin Lab, but has rich and shiny black (or sometimes liver) feathers. The flat-coat is a frolicker. Not suitable for the stale regimen of field trials, he prefers the variety and the independence afforded him by the hunting field.

Formerly the gamekeeper's shooting dog in Great Britain, this dog was born of the same litter as the Lab. The keepers called the long-coated pups flat-coats, and the short-coats Labs. Later the two were selectively bred. It was that simple.

You know English springer spaniels and cocker spaniels came about the same way. In the old days the big pups in the litter were called springers, and the little guys were called cockers. Thus the birth of two separate breeds of gun dogs we have today. And we'll have a story about them coming up.

A MIKE GOULD THINK-ALIKE

Right up front, Ken tells me he'd like to spend some time with Mike Gould and just talk. I intend to set up the meeting.

Then Ken immediately supports Mike's interest in letting young pups grow up to run wild. To have them chase wild birds from the day they can separate the bush.

GOTTA GO HUNTING

Ken tells me, "It's the only way it can be done. You take control guys and early-bird guys," he says, "my experience has been it's so much better if you put birds in first. It's just like kids you know . . . say with music. They learn that a lot better as a child than they do at fifty. And we know languages are that way.

"It's the same for everything about the total hunt, not just birds. I take the pup out in the country as much as I can, get him used to the smells, wade in the water, whatever he wants to do. You can put control on a dog anytime.

"Ten-year-old dogs are going to obedience classes. But you can't put 'country' back in a hunting dog. I was given a dog for training that was two years old, never been out in the field. I had to get her used to walking over stuff, took her to construction sites, pipes, barrels, stairs, so when she came out here to the field, things didn't bother her. She should have had all that as a puppy."

BIRDCRAFT

"I meet guys who put the control in first. And the birds come second. But to me, bird dogs are for birds. That's what their whole life is about.

"Now the control guy is going to say that's stupid . . . heel, sit, stay, is what he wants . . . not getting birds.

"Well, honestly, I think the nose of these dogs has to be developed. Birdcraft has to be developed. Birdiness has to be developed. Just like when we do water work with a dog, we do it in a running river. Every dog can swim in a farm pond, that's not the problem. White water . . . that's where a dog will learn to swim.

"So I'd say a dog can't do both control and birds equally. Disciplined dogs are going to serve you first and then get birds. What I want my dogs to do is get birds first and then, incidentally, I'd like for them to mind me while they're doing it."

THE MECHANICAL DOG

Ken is so unmistakably right here. How many times have I seen it. The boot polisher. The dog belonging to some adult or some kid who lives deep within the city, and can't get to the country, and so spends his or her spare time teaching heel, sit, stay.

The dog becomes a robot. Daily he goes through his dull and meaningless routine. He has no motivation. He has no goal. If only he had a bird. A bird to psyche him, to thrill him, to drive him. See the difference?

That's why many conscientious gun dog breeders today will not sell you a dog unless you can assure them the dog will be hunting.

YOU CAN TRAIN AT HOME

This doesn't mean you can't train at home. It's a matter of emphasis. Obedience leading to good citizenry—such as heel, sit, stay—gets stale if

Ken says, "I'm an 'early bird' guy," as he heels pup following fetch.

there's no objective. I remember in the Marine Corps the rifle range was a lot more exciting and meaningful to me than the parade field.

But Ken tells us how you can train a dog at home with good results. He says, "I had a pup with parvo. So I decided to train her in the living room while I nursed her back to health." Now first off, there ain't many pros training dogs in their house.

Ken tells us, "Well we started simple, but later we advanced even to hand signals. I did all my training on my knees. I'd heel her and cast a baby dummy and send her out, only to whistle her down and give her a hand signal to move her sideways, or as it is said in field trial parlance, give her an over. Then finally I'd let her fetch to hand.

"One of the things we did was seed the living room carpet with little teal decoys. So she was learning to avoid them as she took her hand signals and made her retrieves. Then I got the idea, why not let her pick up the decoys after the training session is over. And so I did.

"The weather got better when spring came, and we went out in the backyard and continued our training. And that yard opened things up quite a bit for us. The flat-coat quickly adapted, and I knew she was going to be a great gun dog.

"Now that she's an all-age dog, when I finish duck hunting with her, I cast her out to pick up each of the decoys.

"People are aghast. 'You can't do that,' they tell me. 'That means during the hunt she will pick up decoys, too.'

"People just don't know the brilliance of a dog. This dog knows the difference between hunting and gathering up after the hunt is over."

SOMETHING HERE, SOMETHING THERE

We've been standing outside a puppy yard at Ken's training grounds. Now we walk toward his kennels. He tells me, "Pigeons are the backbone of training for us. And we shoot them. So the dogs get a lot of birds. They get to retrieve a lot of birds. Gun dogs have that natural energy anyway, why stomp that out of them making them do bumpers?

"When dogs are puppies with us, we want them to get their mouths on everything they can. I've seen this. I've seen an old duck dog who had to learn about pheasants. Not with the dogs we turn out. They know as many game birds as we can provide them."

THE GUN-SHY TAPE

"Oh we have a lot of things we do. I bought a gun-shy audio tape. You know, a symphony playing classical music and then the music gets louder and explosions start and then everything gentles down. And I play that in the whelping bin . . . before the puppies are even born."

There it is again. The same belief that pups in the embryo can decipher sensations. You saw it earlier with Gary Ruppel when he was whistling to his unborn pups. Remember?

Ken goes on explaining, "As they mature, that tape is played while the pups are eating—they wake up to it, they go to sleep with it.

"And once they get out in the dog yard we have all kinds of things out there. Ladders and barrels and ramps and bridges and tunnels. Just everything we can think of. And we move the stuff around. The pups are always getting a different perspective.

"The result of all this is these pups are not afraid of anything."

HANDLING ERROR

"And I'm going to tell you something else," says Ken. He explains in a grave voice, "Before anybody buys one of those electric shock collars, they ought to invest in a home video camera. The problem they think they got to shock the dog to rid him of . . . may be seen on tape as a handling error.

"Like the guy who was saying, 'No,' three times when he was correcting his dog. So why should that dog answer the first no? He knew two more were coming.

"So if a dog is not following directions, if he's not heeding you, you're probably not telling him right.

"That's why if you are going to teach hand signals, you should practice in front of a mirror. See what the dog sees. I'll bet you'll change your stance and the way you move your arms.

"And something else. Anytime you get down on your knees your dog thinks it's love time. Right? So you take him out to a duck blind—which is a sunken pit—and you get down there and now you're even with your dog's face. What's he going to do? That's right. Lick you, jump on you, swipe a big paw across you asking for a loving.

"Well that's distracting when you're trying to shoot ducks. So build yourself a pit blind and get your pup and practice in it. Let him know

Ken says, "Duck hunters should work their dogs out of blinds, then the dog knows you're not getting down there to love him and goes berserk."

there's a difference between your being in that blind and being on your knees in the living room.

"It's like I always say, some of the things we do can cause our own problems. Like getting down in the living room [and then] later fowling up a duck hunt."

THE BIRD FIELD

"But the best thing I do for my pups is put them in a bird field with a whole lot of pinioned pigeons. Let them chase them, and fetch then, and carry them around. Nothing builds birdiness like this."

So where Gary and Mike say let the pups run after wild birds—since they have the land—Ken Osborn, with a more limited venue, maximizes birdiness in a small enclosure and lots of pigeons. Both ways work.

STEERING ARM, PRAISE ARM

Ken's still talking, and I hear him say something I've never heard before. Holding up his left hand he says, "This is my steering arm." Then holding up his right hand he tells me, "This is my praise arm."

Then he says, "Always remember the difference. And here's one way it works. When I love a dog, I don't want to see him pull away from me. So I put my steering hand under his chin to steady him and love him with my praise hand.

"I've been called on that at hunt tests where I've run. They think I've been teaching something with two hands on a dog. I haven't. I'm just praising the dog, settling him. That's all.

"That's how I came up with reaching dogs by cupping my hands. You know, I'd have kibbles in my cupped left hand, and I'd reach in with my right hand and using my fingers take out a kibble and give one to each dog. Well it finally occurred to me all I had to do was cup my left hand and place my right hand in there, and the dogs would attend to whatever lesson I wanted to teach. It works.

"We try to make everything work. Why, we have dogs go home and come back for another session, and the first place they go is right up on the retrieving table. For I feed them up there, give them treats up there, love them up there. That's what you need to do. Make a bad place a good place in their minds."

TRAINING THE CLIENT

"Then you're not finished with a dog until you've trained the client. The pro's job is to make the dog as good as he can be. Then make the client as good as he can be—with his dog. You've got to build that bridge.

"One way to do that is take a green amateur and let him run your all-age dogs. This gives him, or her, confidence to see that they slap a hand signal on and the dog takes it. The handler gets all puffed up, tickled, happy. It works."

THE DISTAFF

About this time we're joined by Ken's wife, Kathie. Kathie is a former show handler, specializing in flat-coat retrievers. She listens to us for a while and then says to me, "You say you want all the dog left in the dog. You don't want it beat out."

"Yes," I tell her, I didn't know she was listening.

"Well that's the way we train. Dogs are motivated, never intimidated. You'll not find any of our gun dogs running in handcuffs. They run free, having their own head, their own self assurance."

Now I'm getting it from both sides. Great, that's what I want to see, a fervor about humane gun dog training.

"But," Kathie says, "I can't make my Ford into a Mercedes. People got to know the same goes for dogs. You can't make a flat-coat into a Lab. Everyone must gauge their training and set their expectations on the breed of dog they've got. A flat-coat just isn't going to look good at a field trial. You've got to take flat-coats hunting. That's where they excel."

Ken speaks up, offering, "That also goes back to the way we train the pups: flat-coats or other. The more you put into a pup's memory bank, the more they have to draw from when they get to be a dog. And they will draw from it. A rich childhood makes a great gun dog. But not a great field trial dog. Because the dog is permitted to offer so little on his own at a field trial."

HAVING LUNCH

The three of us leave the field. The Osborns have offered to take me to Chevy's, possibly the finest Mexican restaurant chain in California. I'm a Tex-Mex nut. If you don't believe it read my book, *How to Hunt Birds With*

Flat-coat in blind shows thin chest, almost setter-like, that makes for speed in the field.

Gun Dogs. Most of my recipes for game birds in there are based on tequila and chili. I don't drink booze nor wine, but sometimes these two ingredients make a fascinating seasoning over a fire.

We sit far too long at Chevy's talking dogs. Finally the place is empty except for us. I'm pleased with the day. Good people, good food.

I realize as I sit there watching the Sacramento River flow by, there are more and more Ken Osborns announcing themselves across America every day. Each trainer who steps forward is another gift to gun dogs.

You've got to have your ear tuned to the novel when talking with pioneers and land-breakers like Ken. I hear him say, "You know we're quick to make a retriever sit before giving a command when he's away from us."

ALWAYS MAKE THE DOG SIT

That's right, we've all whistled Pup down, waited until he was sitting steady, and then given a back- or an overhand signal.

Ken continues, "But we never do it when the dog is right in front of us. And that's what we should be doing. Having the dog sit breaks the behavior we find at fault. Then once the behavior is broken, we can give a command to do what's right."

I'd never thought of it before, but Ken is right.

That's what I like about this new breed of gun dog trainer. They're always thinking, always testing new ideas. In the old days, you know, when a dog came to a trainer, it was demanded the dog fit the trainer's system.

Today's trainer designs a system for each dog. Should the dog have some unique characteristic, the trainer doesn't scuttle him for it. The trainer works around it, or corrects it, or modifies whatever the characteristic is.

And that's because, like we said up front, we're now training with our heads, not our hands. And we are training without pain. So the dog performs because he wants to, not because he has to.

We got lost in our training for several decades, but we're back on track now. We're heading for a bright horizon.

Lance stops deep-woods training to love brace two vizsla pups. (Photo by Donna De Filippis/Dorratz Vizslas)

11

Lance Casper

This trainer's program, and his very life, is based on genetics, early exposure to the vitals, whistle training, and no stress.

Lance Casper of Newton, New Jersey, has been working toward our gun dog training goals for several years. Seemingly propelled by a turbo-assist, this slight-built man maintains a training schedule that's a far cry from his apparent make-up. What I'm talking about is Lance is five feet eight inches, 150 pounds, fifty years old. Yet he will hand-groom clients with their dogs all day (he does this on an hourly basis), then, checking to see how much light shows in the west, hurriedly grab his own dogs and head out hunting.

Clients have been known to say, "You're something else, you know that? Work with dogs all day, then want to take 'em hunting. Where do you get the energy?"

Lance answers, "My dogs have taken a back seat all day and they want to hunt . . . so we're going hunting."

Each trainer highlighted in this book has many characteristics in common. But one *they all share* is their obsession for sensitive dog training. Bringing dogs along with patience and kindness seems to take over one's soul, one's goal, one's essentials. Nothing else becomes so pivotal, so important. It becomes all-consuming, the study of it, the testing of new techniques, the thinking out of new solutions. It is truly a thinking person's undertaking. And a dedicated person's undertaking.

TREATING DOGS SAME AS PEOPLE

And repeatedly I see this among the dog trainers featured in this book. They are the dogs' equal friend. The trainers are not viewed as a human. But a dog person with dog love and a dog to give the love to.

It's a whole new relationship between human and dog. It's based on mutual respect, mutual admiration, mutual concern. The dog is as filled with his love of the human as the human is overcome with his or her love of the dog.

Remember in the last cameo, Ken Osborn said the old-time dog trainer had to keep up a false image of macho. He felt he had to prove he was tough enough "to handle a dog."

Now the criterion is, "Are you sensitive enough to handle a dog?"

Quite a turnaround, huh?

It goes back to something I wrote somewhere a long time ago. I was thinking about the fighter, the man with a perpetual chip on his shoulder. The guy with the curled fist. And I realized, and I wrote, how very much strength it took for that man to uncurl his fists and meet an adversary with open, extended palms.

And that's just about what's happened to dog training.

And you'd think the dog was the benefactor. And he is, but you know the human is, too? As the honky-tonk song goes, and I paraphrase, "I'm going back to a better class of people."

TRAINING

Lance Casper trains on a 660-acre dog club and game preserve. It's a tree-filled venue, so Lance naturally says he sees little value in field trial pointing dogs. Nor does he necessarily specialize in retrievers. Lance says field trial pointers' big casts would be wasted in his tight country. He says, "What value is a dog running big, he'd get nowhere in these trees."

Now couple this with the fact Lance trains essentially the NAVHDA-type dogs. That's the North American Versatile Hunting Dog Association. Remember, Butch went to talk to them.

These people run the shorthair and longhairs and Spinoni and vizslas and pudelpointers and griffons and the rest. These dogs hunt fur and feather, point and fetch, track and trail, and are just flat versatile.

NO-STRESS TRAINING

Lance says, "The vizsla people have especially sought me out because of my no-stress training and the fact vizslas will not respond to a heavy hand."

I ask him to outline his program, and he starts explaining, which he does forthrightly and to the point. For though Lance is soft on dogs, he is hard on himself. He is exact, he measures each word so he won't be misunderstood. And he is a serious man. These dogs, and what he does with them, matter.

NO ABUSE

Lance says, "One cannot train with abuse. You can't train with pain. This is because you find you get a much better response, a much better hunting dog, if you approach him with innate kindness.

"Dogs respond so much better to human contact and to positive reinforcement. I've proven this many times. I've had dogs in here that were strictly kennel dogs, and their owners couldn't believe the turnaround in the dog in a month's time. I'm talking about personalitywise. It was all accomplished in thirty days in a one-to-one bonding process.

"And I've had people who kennel their dogs prior to my training them, and now they're taking the dogs and keeping them in their house. That's what love will get for you."

PUPPIES

"On puppies," says Lance, "I start basic coming to the whistle in the yard. I'll whistle, slap my leg, and run. When they chase me and catch up with me, I'll get down on my knees and gather them all up in my arms. I don't care how many of them there are; three, four, whatever. I'll bundle them all up close to me.

"When they all get to me, I tell them, 'Good, come,' and 'That's a good puppy.' I want to instill in them that coming to me is the best thing that ever happened to them. Before I turn them loose, I give them the release word. So now what I'm ingraining in them is they are not to take off and go anywhere until I allow them to."

"What's your release word?" I ask.

And Lance replies, "'Free,' that's what I tell them. But I have one bitch I do have a special release for."

"What's that?"

"Spaghetti Os."

RETRIEVING

I clear my throat and inquire, "How do you get your dogs to retrieve?"

"I sit them in front of me and I ask them to fetch, and I help open their mouth, and I place the dummy in it. Then I say 'give' and take it out. That's it."

"And it works?"

"It works. It just takes longer than it does when inflicting pain. But of course that's not an alternative."

"You are probably very good at reading a dog," I tell him.

He answers, "I can do it. But when I try to teach people to do it, that's difficult. Some are okay, but others are out in left field. Yet, I find that women are able to administer praise and affection, where men tend to be too cold. I see this in a dog immediately.

"When I read a dog, I cue on the ears, the eyes, the head, the tail, the body posture . . . everything from the tip of their nose to the tip of their tail."

NEVER TIED

When I ask him if there's anything else unusual in his training Lance says, "I never put a lead on a dog. He always runs free. Goodbye-dogs need a check cord, but I don't have goodbye-dogs. Consequently I attract people who love their dogs and want to bond with them. That's the type of people who seek me out as a trainer."

Then he offers, "You know, dogs have taught me a lot about life in the area of unconditional love. No matter what kind of mood you're in, or what kind of day you've had, that dog is there for you. Even if you're having a tough time with that particular dog, in five minutes that dog has forgotten all about your tough time, and that dog is right back working with you.

"Dogs for the most part are very forgiving creatures. You can work with a dog or a pup and have a tough little session, and five minutes later . . .

*Lance Casper kneels down with two German shorthair pointers bearing the kennel name Muddy Foot. (*Photo by John Norton)

"Just a minute, let me say it this way. If you're having a problem with a dog in the learning process, you've just got to stop. Just stop and walk away and let the puppy walk away. And the two of you just cheer up and come back and do something else."

NO BADGERING

"I can't stand for someone to badger a dog. Continually harp on a dog. I taught dog obedience for many years under the premise that a dog learns by constant repetition. Well the dog also becomes extremely bored when trained that way. So I prefer to train with consistency, not so much repetition, and I like to put the training in the middle of fun time."

"What do you mean by fun time?"

"Let's say you're working a two-year-old dog. Give him a hug, toss a dummy for him, do something that isn't structured. I'll just let them run and get the dummy and tell them, 'great guy, having fun?'"

Then I ask Lance, "What's the most important aspect of dogs, or dog training, in your program?"

ONCE AGAIN, BREEDING

"Breeding," he insists. "That's my whole concept of dogs. There're so many poorly bred dogs out there. And yet with proper breeding—here let me show you. See this eleven-week-old pup? I had him pointing birds the other day. And when that bird ran, that pup circled the bird . . . he did it each time the bird tried to get away. He never chased the bird directly. No, he circled the bird and held it. That's one of my shorthair pups out of my own kennel."

COME OUT HUNTING

"I've never bred and whelped a pup that didn't come out hunting. And because of that I've had clients say to me, 'No matter what dogs you choose to breed, you just seem to have an eye to know what pair to put together.'

"Well, I tell them, that's all just intuition. And picking the positive point out of the dog to pick up . . . a weaker point in another one. I want to see basic hunting in the sire and the dam. I want to see them point, and quarter, and retrieve naturally. And that's what breeding is all about. Looking at your breeding stock, knowing what you're seeing and wanting, and putting the two best prospects together."

The man laughs and says, "One good pup proves nothing. But a series of great pups proves everything. And I've been lucky to produce just that."

WANTS GOD-MADE DOGS

"Is that about it?" I ask.

Lance answers with a wink, "I don't want to breed a dog that I have to put the dog in him. I want to breed a dog that God put the dog in him. By that I mean I want natural ability, not something a trainer put in that wasn't there to start with."

I wink back and tell Lance, "I think I've heard that before."

But before I can say goodbye, Lance raises his voice, saying, "It's necessary you use only your presence to train. Your love, your soft hands. If there's an older dog that has a bad problem and needs correction, I will collar him, so if he breaks, I can put him back from the spot he left. And I do that by picking him up.

"Everything from then on has to be positive reinforcement. I prefer to work with the dogs so they can understand right from wrong. And the only way they can equate this is by reinforcement. Not by correction and discipline.

"And what do I mean by reinforcement? I pick the dog up and put him back from where he left. Right? If he stands there I praise him, if he moves again, I pick him up again and put him back where he left. There's no criticism. There's no discipline. No punishment. There's only reinforcement. Understand?"

I have to smile to myself, never have I met a more conscientious or hard-driven trainer. I tell him, softly, "Yes Lance, I understand."

Bob holds Elhew pup for kiss. He says, "Training is a scientific art."

12

Bob Wehle

Bob Wehle is the top gun dog breeder of the twentieth century, and in my estimation, of all time. His line of Elhew pointers has so refined and advanced the breed that puppy buyers now write Bob to say things like, "I am very disappointed. I bought an eight-week-old pup from you and was so looking forward to training it. But my pup came trained."

Bob Wehle is a majority of one. He goes his own way, has his own say, does things his own way. And the results are always better than we've seen before. Born to fortune, Wehle's business ability made life more fortunate still. But the money was never spent for glitter. It went for the most part to Wehle's beloved English pointers. It went to building the most famous gun dog kennel in America (Elhew located in Midway, Alabama, and Henderson, New York), and to producing the finest string of gun dogs the world has ever seen.

Now let me pause. We've read of eleven gun dog notables, and each of them in some way has alluded to breeding as the primary essential in great gun dogs. One trainer emphasized natural ability. That's breeding. Another pointed out sensitivity training wasn't possible until we had a better breed of dog. And so it's gone. Now we meet a man who knew all this sixty years ago and set out to provide just such a dog.

THE OLD POINTERS

English pointers have been known as marauders, self-willed raiders whose carnal instinct would make them kill two cats between coveys, then bolt

Author (left) and Bob Wehle pose with pointer dam. (Photo by Bill Berlat)

to the next county and wipe out a chicken coop.

Wehle put an end to all this nonsense. Wehle gives us an English pointer so bright and polite he could be the concierge in a plush hotel.

So realize, Wehle's genius is genetics: breeding. He's proven it with Holstein cows, thoroughbred race horses, and English pointers. But doing it and getting him to talk about it are two different things, for he sidesteps honor—though a member of the Field Trial Hall of Fame, you'll not find the certificate on his wall.

LINE BREEDING

I stay with Bob several days at his southern holdings to draw him out. Wehle is a tall man with straight carriage, silver hair, and a tangle of eyebrows that practically cover eyes the color of waxed saddle leather. Bob speaks slowly, with measured thought. His voice is low, but I hear him say, "I don't think building a bird dog line is that complicated. There's no long, complicated formula to breed anything. I think it's line breeding . . . stay within the family. That's all line breeding is. Just the proper selection of the individuals."

The man's cooking supper (it's a special thing with him), and he throws the pans on the stove to clatter. He gathers fresh produce from his greenhouse each day and whomps up a meal. Wehle is a gracious host, but it's hard to hear him amid banging steel. He says, "I think quantity is very important. I think if you have one bitch and you are trying to produce a pure string of pointers, and your neighbor has ten bitches and he's after the same thing, he's going to beat you.

IT'S ALL VOLUME

"So I keep a lot of breed bitches. It's all volume . . . obviously I don't need 150 puppies a year. It's more aggravation to me than anything else to have that many dogs and have to merchandise them. It makes a very commercial operation out of my kennels. But I don't know how else to do it. I haven't the heart to dispose of those puppies. Oh no, I can't do that. So my only method is what I'm doing. Breed them, keep the 2 percent I want, and sell the rest."

Wehle's love for his dogs is all-pervasive. Never have I seen such clean kennels, such innovative equipment. Entering one of his four whelping bins, he turns to look at my shoes and asks, "You been in any other kennel lately?" If I had been, there was a tray of disinfectant (or something) for me to walk through.

Bob fights disease, and he feeds the latest formulas in nutrition. And his dog training techniques are based totally on intimacy, never intimidation.

WHO'S MORE IMPORTANT?

Bob tells me, "You see, all matings don't nick [a word that means the mix produces something special]. You'll hear people say, 'Well, the bitch is more important than the male.' I just don't believe that. I believe that there are important female lines and there are important male lines. And I think this is well demonstrated in other breeding . . . in Holstein cattle for example.

"You can well trace out cow families . . . where the female prevails. Now those females in that strong cow family will reproduce, and they are probably a lot more important than the males they are breeding them to. But by the same token, there are male lines like Bold Ruler in the horse line. His sire produced; he produced; his sons produced. It was a strong male line. So breed one of those horses to a mare, and you get a dominant male line. And there I would say the male is more important.

"But you simply can't say the female is more important . . . it depends on who you are dealing with."

THE O'RILEYS

I sit on a high stool before the kitchen counter. Wehle measures spices by dragging a thick index finger into and out of the jar. As he's doing this he says, "You can do it with humans. We had a family of . . . oh, let's call them O'Rileys . . . back in Albion, New York. And it was a big family. And one of the O'Rileys worked for us. Why, he had a brother who was very high up in the Roosevelt administration. But all the O'Rileys came from Albion—a big, big clan.

"Why, I could tell an O'Riley three blocks away. I mean, really. It was a dominant male line. There is no mistake about it. And while I'm in some little town fox hunting in Ireland, some nineteen-year-old kid walks down the street. And so help me . . . I looked at him and said, 'You're name has to be O'Riley.' His name was O'Riley. A strong line, a male line. Had to be. People don't believe this, but this kid could have been sired by the guy who worked for us. He was the image of his son. They looked like twins, and there they were two thousand miles apart."

Let me interrupt here. Bob Wehle is fascinating. He tells stories like this all the time. What a life he's had. He's walked with swanks and gatekeepers, but prefers to sit on a kennel table and spend the day with rustics. He loves handcraftsmanship. He's even building an iron forge on his property. And he's a world-class sculptor, an author, a philanthropist, an art collector. It goes on and on. But he is not accomplished in everything: His wife, Gatra, beats him in pool.

Bob is also an interior decorator. He'll pick up a handful of flowers and let them dry, then hang them on the door. Beside the entrance to his kitchen is a tote sack of pecans. You walk out, reach down, scoop a hand-

A master sculptor, Wehle recently donated a life-size bronze of his National Shooting Dog Champion, Snakefoot, to the Field Trial Hall of Fame.

ful for your pocket, and you're fixed for the day. Yes, Bob has his life in order. A simple life for a complex man. A man who shares everything he has, but his most precious gift is his genius.

Bob has kept talking while I've visited with you, and now he's saying, "So you run into that everywhere. Now Elhew Marksman was a strong male line. Elhew Jungle, Elhew Huckleberry . . . you know . . . strong male line." [These three pointers were all national champions.] Bob goes on to say, "And there are other great animals, but with those animals that greatness stops. They never can reproduce."

BLUE HEN

"Have you ever heard the term 'blue hen'?" Bob asks. (Every time he asks me a question it's got the word 'blue' in it. He recently asked me if I knew of Bluenose. Of course I didn't. But a month later, grouse hunting in

Nova Scotia, there it was, the ship 'Bluenose.' How would a guy from landlocked Kansas know a ship named Bluenose?)

Bob says, "A 'blue hen' is a thoroughbred term for a mare that has produced a multitude of winners. No matter who you breed her to, she produces a great horse. Well, I've been using the term for thirty years. Because in my lifetime I've probably had five blue hens in dogs. I could breed them to a fence post and get good pups, really. It made no difference who I bred her to, she had great puppies. And every once in a while you run into a blue hen. I've got one in the making right now."

THE DRAG OF THE RACE

Wehle asks me to set the table, and I do as Wehle brings the food and inspects the spread. He tells me, "A lot of people don't understand about breeding any animal . . . about what I call the drag of the race.

"You can call it whatever you want. It's a tendency toward mediocrity. It's a fact that if you take five dogs, either of one breed or five different breeds, and you put them on an island and let them breed promiscuously, it would only be a question of time before the offspring would revert back to a common dog, probably wolflike in nature. The color would be wolflike, and all that. And I don't care what you start with, that will happen. In other words," he says, his voice building now for he's warming to his subject, "the nature of things denies excellence. Because there's always this drag on the race. It's always withering away, and no matter how far you proceed, you lose something each time you gain.

"So it's not good enough to breed to a mediocre dog. You have to breed to a dog that's extra special. I don't know how to tell you this without referring to my own dogs, but to me King is a little above average; he's not ordinary. That's why he's going to be a sire for me. Tycoon, the dog I showed you, he's above average. And I think he's not a run-of-the-mill dog; he's not common. He's not ordinary at all. And I think what you have to do is concentrate constantly on building upon these above-average dogs. If you just breed mediocrity, you're just going to go down. And I think that's why there's a lot of bad dogs in the country." He pauses and asks, "You want some turnip greens?"

I take the greens and feel them bite my inner cheeks; they have a pungency akin to mustard. I ask Wehle, "To you, what's above average in a bird dog?"

Top: *Bob releases quail from pen . . .*
Bottom: *. . . then works pointer behind house.*

THE INTELLIGENT DOG

Wehle concentrates on his food a while, then answers. "The intelligent dog. Of course, he has all the natural attributes, which are tenacity, the desire to find game, the ability to point, the ability to scent game at distances. But what separates dogs, from my point of view, is their intelligence.

"And I would like to think that the dogs we are breeding are reasonably smart. But isn't this a natural happenstance? *Because the smarter dog is the dog that's the most appealing, and that's the dog you're going to end up with as a breeding animal.* And if you do that generation after generation, then you've got something. And I can separate the intelligent dogs from those that are not at a very early age. If you just spend enough time with them and watch them . . . you can see the most precocious dogs. Just simple little things. *Some dogs always know how to go through a gate; some dogs can never figure it out.* That's intelligence."

Days later I mention this to my wife, Dee. This thing of Bob selecting intelligence as that factor which makes us most appreciate an animal. And we both agree he's right. We have a wee bitch named Candy that's our pride and joy. Dee says it's because of her "spark." She says, "It's because we are so thrilled at seeing her succeed." And Dee's right. Thanks, Bob, for having us look closely at something we've not noticed before.

THE DOG THAT PLEASES YOU

"So you subconsciously gravitate to the more intelligent dog," adds Wehle, "and the dogs that have the personality that pleases you. And if you continue to breed that sort of a dog, that's what you'll end up with. The performance is pretty much man made from that time on . . . if you've got a dog with natural attributes and the intelligence and disposition, then you've got the perfect shooting dog . . . because you make him the perfect shooting dog."

I chew my turnip greens and reach for a glass of water.

"Anything else?" asks Wehle.

I can only say, "What's for dessert."

Wehle chuckles, and arches his right eyebrow as he looks at my greens. He's got so much bramble in those eyebrows a quail could hunker down in there.

One time I grabbed a fly rod and took off around the world—fishing. I remember seeking out the Oracle of Delphi in Greece. In ancient times, a girl sat on a three-legged stool over a hole in a huge stone floor and gave prophecy. Kings and noblemen and warriors and scholars came from thousands of miles around to hear her words.

At Delphi, as a curious writer would, I made inquiry. And by the time I left, I'd learned there was a sulfurous stench that came up through that hole in the stone, and the girl, being on a three-legged stool and bending over the hole, would become quite woozy and hallucinate. I say to Bob, "Do you think they have turnip greens in Greece . . . since what you've said is brilliant."

He does not answer but looks at me with a vague expression of, "Are you nuts?"

Well folks, you've just sat at a table outside Midway, Alabama, and heard the most brilliant dissertation on gun dog breeding that was ever stated, and possibly ever will be. And stated by the finest gun dog breeder the world has ever seen.

Bob Wehle is such a master of understatement. You'll get lulled to comfort since the man is so soothing, and then you'll not realize how brilliant everything he said really is.

Join us for dog talk and greens and maybe a three-legged stool next time you're in the county, ya hear now?

Mark Sullivan sets a horse well. Adorned for the hunt, his dog takes one backward glance before entering the bottoms.

13

Mark Sullivan

We have a false image about coon hunters. They're imagined as good ol' boys with a jug of homemade, a bonfire, a sad-eyed dog rousted from under the porch, and a pair of overalls with only one shoulder strap snapped. As I make my rounds putting ink on sporting dogs and the men who love them, I find the most intense, interesting, and informed are the coon hunters. Now doesn't that twist your wisdom?

Listen to Mark Sullivan and verify what I say. Coon men analyze their sort and their sport and their dogs—and become both serious and scholarly in the pursuit of their mania. And mania is what it is.

THE COON HUNTER

Folks kept telling me about Mark Sullivan. Said he lived over in Pocahantas, Tennessee, owned his own meat cutting business at thirty-four, and liked to hunt coon. And that all proved to be true. But that's not how I found him. I met a living encyclopedia titled *Everything You Ever Wanted to Know About Coon Hunting: If You Wanted To Know It Right*.

Now I've accompanied each of you meeting a lot of outdoorsmen and -women. And we've found most of them at the top of their field. And ain't nobody knows more about coon hunting than Mark. He's been at it since he was twelve, when he used to climb trees and shake the coons out, until today, when he's the state of the art in his sport.

A slab-built guy, with a hawkish nose, intensive stare, and close-set ears, Mark talks slowly but thoroughly (as he does everything). And, as he tells his outspoken and up-front story, you feel the joy he has in just being him.

A HARD HUNTER

I ask Mark, "Why is it all you guys go crazy about coon hunting? Why is that sport so addictive?"

"Oh we don't go crazy," he protests, "it takes a lot of time and a lot of hours to make a good dog, and everybody wants to have the best dogs, you know.

"I've been divorced twice, and I'm not going to say all of it was coon hunting, but it had a lot to do with it.

"I think if a woman loves a man, she doesn't mind him going coon hunting two or three nights a week. I just always been a hard hunter, and I've got a girlfriend now, and she knows that when I get ready to go hunting, I'm going hunting, and I'm going hunting tonight.

"That one wife of mine told me I had to quit coon hunting and quit fooling with those horses. And I said okay. But after two months I couldn't do it. And I told her, if you don't love me for what I am and what I like to do there'll always be trouble between us.

"You see coon hunting . . . it's not that a man goes crazy about it. It's just coon hunting: you're gone at night, and your wife don't like to be left at home. You end up leaving them regularly, and they end up finding somebody they think will stay with 'em."

I tell him, "I rest my case."

And he says, "Huh?"

"Never mind," I say, then ask, "Why don't you have a jumping mule?"

THIS THING ABOUT MULES

"'Cause I love to hunt the bottoms, and a mule's feet are too small and stick in the mud. A horse got a bigger foot plus he's a lot easier to train. People always talk about the jumping mule; that's the hillbilly idea of coon hunting. But my horse jumps. I just take him up to a four-strand barbed-wire fence, dismount, and take the long reins with me, then stand beside him and say, 'Get up.' He sticks his nose out as if to measure the height and then up he goes and over."

If you've never seen this, folks, it's fascinating. A coon hunting mule or horse can stand flatfooted and clear these fences. It's part of the nostalgia and mystique of the sport. And why the horse? It beats walking.

"But no need for my horse to jump," explains Mark, "since I hunt the bottoms and there's no barbed wire down there."

TREEIN' WALKERS

"You a good dog trainer?" I ask Mark.

"Not necessarily a good puppy trainer. But I stay with treein' Walkers cause they're usually a quick-strike dog and a fast locator on the tree, plus they can have a good, loud mouth.

"I generally start mine about four months old and drag a coon hide around and get 'em to playing . . . and then I turn them loose, and they chase after it, and I hang it up and let them tree on it. And some of them will and some of them won't.

"Then when the season comes at about eight to ten months old, and they've got a lot of that puppy out of them. I already used a coon in a rolling cage, and I let them get after that. And then I'll hang it up in a tree and get 'em to treeing on it.

"You're really not supposed to keep a coon, you know, but I'll catch one with a live trap, and after training the pups, I'll take him back to the same spot I found him and let him go . . . with the pups all chasin' along behind him.

"The thing is, you know, you can teach a dog to run a coon up a tree, but you can't make him bark after he gets there. And if he don't bark, you ain't got nothin'."

HUNTING WITH AN OLDER DOG

"Finally I shoot a coon out during season for the young dogs and try to get 'em started good. Get them excited.

"When I start hunting them in earnest, I put them in the woods with a good, settled, middle-aged to old-aged dog. Then after they start treein' on their own, I hunt them by themselves.

"And then on a hunt we pull the pups away from the tree and squawl a coon out of the tree and let him take off again. And we put those pups back on him hot and let them run him and tree him again."

(About this squawling, I'll explain. Some coon are nervous, and you can identify them on a limb by their looking around and moving about. You squawl, and they are likely to climb down the trunk and leap to the ground if you make a raucous squawling noise and push the coon down with your flashlight following his tail. It's a God-awful sound, and its effect is to give the pups the chance to tree the coon once again, which is a very efficient training method.)

"Also," explains Mark, "on training them pups, you can pick up the dog and stand him up on the tree, excite him with your voice. Then eventually a pup starts seein' what your seein'."

SEEIN' WHAT YOU'RE SEEIN'

I like the power and simplicity of that statement: Mark's way of telling us the dog is learning his business plus bonding with his handler. So I repeat, "That pup starts seein' what you're seein'." This could apply to all gun dogs.

"And something else," adds Mark. "I always tie a pup up when I get to the tree where he's taken a stand. If he's not interested, and he's not really treeing, I find out. Because if you don't, you may develop a dog that wants to run but not tree. And he'll stop at any old tree and lie to you."

LYIN' TO YOU

"I had a buddy who had a female dog that loved to run deer. But when she got tried of running it, she would go to a tree . . . even if there were nothing in it. She'd be sayin', 'I'm, working boss,' when she wasn't working at all.

"Then there's the other thing. A young dog gets up to about three years old, and he's treein' good, but you see that he's missing a lot of things. They tree too quick. The coon might have rubbed his tail on that tree. So the dog stops right there. He's got to learn better than that. He's got to know when the coon actually treed."

FEEDING THE COON

"Of course," says Mark, "you have to feed your coon if you want any to train on. It's training season during the summer, you know, and so you do a couple of things. I put a five-gallon bucket with mixed corn and dog food in it. And I just stir it up and have a hole in the bottom of the side of the pail. Put a piece of PVC pipe in there so the coon can stick his paw in and rake it out. Then you run a piece of metal around the bottom of the pail because if you don't, and that pail runs dry, the coon will eat out the bottom.

"You can also put these buckets up in a tree and put a little limb there just right for them to stand on and eat.

"Then you take and put your corn down in the bottoms in the edge of the mush water and mash it down in the ground, and the coon'll just dig it up after it sours. They like that. And the deer would eat it fresh, but they won't eat it sour. So that way you keep it all for your coon.

"And then you also know where to take your dogs depending on the time of the year. In the spring you go to the bottoms, because you've got the coon eatin' frogs, and tadpoles, and crawfish. Then in the fall you go to the hills for the acorns are falling down."

"I wonder how that can be," I ask, "since I always heard coon have to wash what they eat."

"Yea," confirms Mark, "but it ain't washin'. I understand the coon don't have any saliva glands, so they need moisture to lubricate the swallowing of their food. And even on acorns up in the hills, they can take it to the creek and eat it."

"I'll be," I say in marvel.

A BAG OF CORN

Mark keeps on talking, "Another thing I do is like last night, I took a fifty-pound bag of corn to my bottoms and just poured it out in two different spots in the water. Then I took my foot and smashed it in. That's how you get coon to train a dog."

Mark's still talking as he mounts his horse, with a leash on his dog. And with all that equipment hanging about his body, he starts out for the night. He doesn't want to be impolite, but he really must be going.

I think as I stand there and watch him leave, if anybody wanted to learn to coon hunt, this would be the guy to go with. I wonder if he'd take anyone along. It sure would be worth whatever he charged to see the world of coon hunting through his eyes, astride one of his horses, behind one of his hounds.

WHAT WE'VE CONFIRMED

Hound training is ageless. It goes back to cavemen chasing mastodons. And what was practiced then was the only precedent when it came to training later classes of dogs. So many different breeds were subsequently trained the way hounds were trained.

That's why we have this concept of the older dog training the younger dog. It's the mainstay of hound training. So much so that when I was a kid I used to wonder, "Who trained the first old hound?" and, "What did they train him with?"

Also, we're introduced to pack hunting. And we have the trainer keeping the dog excited in order to keep him interested.

And when Mark tells us, "We want the dog to start seein' what we're seein'," he's telling us, *"We're bonded."*

Mark likewise reveals, "It takes a long time to make a good dog. And everybody wants a good dog."

We all know that, now.

Maybe we didn't know that when we started this book. But we know it now. And we know something else. Those coon hunters out there running in the moonlight aren't hicks. They're disciplined hunters and serious dog trainers, and they know their dog, their game, and their quarry. And they know them all well.

Matter of fact, and you'll not have heard this before, the most expensive gun dogs running are coon dogs. One can cost you as much as forty thousand dollars. Matter of fact, coon hounds have gotten so expensive they're now syndicated like racehorses. And you thought they weren't worth much since all they did was snore under the front stoop.

And why so expensive? Two reasons. First, in competition they run for a purse and the purses have gotten big. And second, like Mark says, "It takes a long time to make a good one."

A downcast pointer (who doesn't like the falling rain) strikes weak pose before Al Brenneman.

14

Al Brenneman

The Bible says there's nothing new under the sun. But there's this fact:
Sometimes what is very old is very new. We join a man of this description
right now.

Do you remember the poem about the fiddle at auction and nobody
would bid? Then an old man walked forward, picked up the fiddle, and
played a tune. When he was finished, the bids skyrocketed. You see the
fiddle had become a violin . . . *in The Master's Hands.*

So it is with eighty-eight-year-old Al Brenneman of Frankewing, Tennessee. Al apprenticed to the most innovative gun dog trainer of all time,
Er Shelley of Columbus, Mississippi. Er was the first man ever to train
on pen-raised and planted birds, the first man to ever make commercial
dog food, the only man I ever heard of who traded two bird dogs for an
estate, and the man who trained and hunted millionaire Paul Rainey's
fifty coon hounds on lions in Africa.

THE MARKET GUNNER

That was Al Brenneman's beginning. But not quite. When Al was ten
years old (in 1918) in Columbus Junction, Iowa, he used cur dogs to retrieve ducks he shot with a borrowed 12-gauge, lever-action shotgun, on
the Cedar, Iowa, and Mississippi Rivers. In fact, Al was a ten-year-old
market gunner, selling his take for one dollar each at the Elks club in
Muscatine. The game wardens winked an eye in his direction, saying, "He's
just a boy." But in truth, Al was a harvesting machine.

Later, in 1937, Al apprenticed to Er Shelley, then went out on his own. He immediately became known as a trainer of problem dogs. The pros would send their misfits who had potential to Al to cure of some "incurable" problem. Al's specialty was gun-shyness.

You can't say Al is wordy. No way. The fact is he's thorough. It takes a long time for Al to explain things. Plus, there are men who are smart in complicated things, but Al is a genius in common sense. He thinks dog. He reads dog. He talks dog.

Listen as we visit.

THE CHAIN GANG

We're standing in Al's barn, out of the rain, with his pet cattle peering through the door at us, and Al's telling me, "You see I've got a chain out here fifty feet long like a trot line." This is a chain staked to earth at each end with eighteen-inch drop chains spaced sixty-six inches apart along its length. Al continues, "We put the problem dog in the middle of the chain with two bold dogs immediately to each side.

"Then I'll plant a bird, and my helper will take a dog out to work on a forty-foot check cord. Now these bold dogs know what's going to happen, and they see the working dog coming in, and they start barking. And what they're doing is cheering the new dog up. Then the working dog goes on point, and these bold dogs back him on the chain gang. The gun shy don't know what's going to happen, and he's looking out here cause there's action.

"Now when the helper grooms the working dog up on point I go out there, flush the bird, and shoot it. The working dog goes out there and retrieves it. I look at the gun-shy dog, and he's scared. He turns around and looks the other direction. He don't want to see that. We humans do the same thing, you know. We do."

THE POOR GUN SHY

"Anyway, I don't pay any attention to this gun shy. I let him suffer. Because there is nothing you can do for him at that time. Now I throw the bird about and let the working dog retrieve it . . . ever getting closer to the gun-shy dog. Finally I throw the bird between the gun shy's feet. He don't want to see that.

"Now these two bold dogs to each side are rattling that chain and really jerking the gun shy about. Then we work another dog the same way. And this gun shy is getting pretty sick, maybe . . .

"Well that goes on for five to ten days. Then you see this gun shy start peeking at the working dog and his bird. But when he sees the bird go up, he'll turn and look the other way. Then we'll wait a few more days . . . every dog is different. Pretty soon though we throw the bird to the gun shy, and he just lays there, but the bold dogs are really shaking him up. They want that bird. Finally you see the gun shy looking, and when the gun fires he says, 'Where did the bird fall?' Then you know you're winning."

HE ACTUALLY SMELLED IT

"Now you throw the bird in and maybe the gun shy will smell it. Day after day you keep this up, and pretty soon the gun shy is the one that's lunging. And these dogs are roughing him up, and the gun shy wants to fight them. That's what we want to see. That sixty-six-inch space between drop chains keeps the dogs from closing in a fight.

"Now the gun shy is lunging for a couple of days and wanting to do the same work as the working dog. Then I'll lay the gun shy up a couple of days, then throw the bird to him. He'll grab it up or bump it around. So I say, well let's work him.

"And the helper will take the gun shy out and bring him *upwind* so he can't smell the bird. I want this to be a surprise. Then I go out and kick around a little to excite the gun shy, and he's happy, because he's going to see some action.

"Then I flush the bird and the helper lets the gun shy go, and he chases the bird away. *I do not shoot.*"

BREAKING ON WING AND SHOT, HURRAY!

"Then pretty soon, another day or two, we let the gun shy smell the bird and then we kick it out and the dog's running in pursuit as fast as he can. *I shoot* and drop the bird right in front of the gun-shy dog. [You going to be able to shoot like this when you're eighty-eight? I'm not.]

"Now that dog may jump in and try to eat the bird, or retrieve the bird, or you never know what's going to happen. *But he can do no wrong.* If he eats it that's all right. He's not here to be trained to retrieve. Then I get plenty of dead birds, and I scatter them all around. And pretty quick it's surprising how he'll quit chewing them. You know he's got so many he can't eat 'em all anyway.

"We keep taking him out, not shooting, and letting him chase the fly-away birds. Finally I shoot a bird for him, and that tickles him. We keep that up for maybe a week. Then I'll take a double barrel out. I flush the bird, and the gun shy chases, and I pull the trigger, and I won't knock the bird down on purpose. Then right away I'll fire again and hit the bird. And the dog keeps going because the bird's falling. He's paying no attention to the gunshots."

THE GUN IS GOOD

"Now the gun shy is on the chain, and there's no bird out, no dog working. We're just standing around like people do. I stand twenty feet away. I fire the gun. And the gun shy just looks around. The gun's good to him now, you see?"

US AMATEURS

"In the old days he would have turned the other way. And we keep this up a couple of days. And it beats the devil how quick he'll understand the gun is part of this whole game. And now he's bold about it. We've won. But the trouble with so many of us . . . us amateurs . . . you might say, is we get in a hurry. We want to do today like it should be done and the dog shows some promise, so tomorrow we [speed the training] up about two weeks, compared with what the trainer would do.

"Then I take the dog out to where I know there's a couple of coveys of birds. And I go walking and let him hunt 'em and find 'em. He'll stagger over them. And he'll run over them, and that excites him, and I'll just stand there for a minute after that happens. Let him smell around and dig in the brush and maybe run after the singles.

"Later I'll fire when he gets the covey up. The dog leaps to fetch the bird up. Our gun-shy dog has now been cured. He loves the gun because that gets him the bird, and the bird is the most exciting thing he's ever seen in all his life.

"This dog can now be sent back to the professional trainer to polish

Al Brenneman stopped short in barn; looks like he could still win two falls out of three.

up for the big field trial circuit. The dog's been saved. He can accomplish now."

THERE'S NO SUN UP IN THE SKY

Well, folks, the rain won't let up—and this barn's leaking. It's rained seven out of the past ten days. Tennessee can be that way. So Al and I, in company with Wilson Dunn of Grand Junction, Tennessee, founder of the Bird Dog Foundation and owner of Dunn's Fearless Bud, the 1990 national bird dog champion, forego coffee in the rustic house where Al lives. No way to run there without getting soaked. So we keep talking in the barn.

NO TRAINING PISTOL

Al tells us, "Now a rifle or a pistol in training can make a dog gun-shy.

Those two weapons make a cracking sound. But a shotgun goes 'Ba-woom.' That Ba-woom becomes a part of the dog's life, the fun part. It means action; it means birds; it means praise for a job well done. But not a crack. Stay away from that crack. Train only with a 20-gauge shotgun in the beginning. Let the dog know only that one Ba-woom sound."

A REVIEW

Now let's see what happened in the telling of this story. Go back to our standard. We learned there that dogs can be positioned to self train. That's what we saw with Al's chain gang. And the standard tells us nothing can train a dog like another dog. That was certainly the case on the chain. And we're also told in the standard about the value of a pack of dogs. Al could have put ten dogs on that chain, and each would have made it's own contribution.

All this is borne out with eighty-eight-year-old Al Brenneman running us through his cure for gun-shyness.

Note too, this gun-shy dog was never touched by the handler. Never hurt. Never trained with pain. He was, matter of fact, trained with Al's head. Remember, "Train with your head, not your hand."

Now we should recognize there was psychological pain inflicted by the gun-shy dog on himself. And that's a tenet in the standard I've not mentioned until now.

There are training drills where the dog controls how much pain he wants to bear. And I'm talking here of self-inflicted pain. Soon as that dog lets his milk down on the chain gang—he's off of it. The dog's in charge of his own fate.

Do you like that?

I do.

So thank you, Al, for taking us youngsters through your drill. Thanks for showing us the power of dogs training dogs.

And before shoving off there's one more thing Al taught us on this visit. You can only train a dog for one thing at a time. Remember that. And while you're training for one result, ignore all other behavior, good or bad.

Al did that, remember? He ignored the dog eating the bird. Curing that is a job for a force fetch specialist. Al's job was to cure the dog of gun-shyness. Remember this. This is very important.

And in closing I'll give you one more tenet for our standard. You can never solve a gun dog problem without creating another. So never create a problem in the first place.

That's right. Whenever you solve gun-shyness the Al Brenneman way, you're likely to develop a dog that eats birds.

And I'm going to assure you of something else. When you are curing the dog of eating birds, you're going to create another problem. That's a truth of dog training that can be engraved in stone: You never solve one problem without creating another.

Bob Wehle talks to dog on love bench prior to training session.

15

Bob Wehle, Revisited

I'm researching a dog named Dr. Blue Willing. And this gets me to think-
ing of Bob Wehle with his blue-hen dams and his Bluenose schooner. So I
drop back by Alabama and ask Bob how his success in breeding fits into
the new humane training. How it fits into our standard.

It's sundown, the time of long shadows outside Midway, Alabama. There's
a hush of wind in the tall pines, a muted call of mating Canadian geese
down on a nearby pond. The last of the songbirds dust themselves on the
packed dirt drive. Bob Wehle and I sit on the lanai of his dog trot. What's
that? A dog trot? A lanai?

Sure. A lanai is the Hawaiian word for porch. The immortal English
setter fancier, Admiral "Doc" Lyons, and I would sit on his lanai for hours
and talk dogs and dog books. The word lanai seems to fit this paradise.
And a dog trot is a Dixie dirt-farmer's house where the kitchen is to one
side and the living quarters to another. So if the kitchen burns, the owner
has a place to live to rebuild it. Between the two rooms is a long hallway
that funnels the breeze. The dogs lie there; it's called a dog trot.

Wehle's is made of rough-out wood, painted washtub gray, hidden
under foliage. It is the southern home of Elhew kennels, having its sixti-
eth birthday this year. That place where the finest string of English pointers the world has ever seen has been produced.

ENTER THE YANKEE
Now I've never told this story before but it tickles me. It's so like Bob.

Bob Wehle came into this Alabama backroad country several years ago, and through various gatekeepers the locals learned this New York moneyfeller was going to build a show place.

Well the folk thereabouts imagined a Corinthian-columned manse with balcony, winding drive, magnolia trees, matched fireplaces, winding staircase, and endless whitewashed stables. They imagined another Tara from *Gone With the Wind*.

Bob, being an artist, toured the country and sketched drawings of what he envisioned. When he eventually showed them to his dinner hosts and hostesses, some may have been horrified. I wasn't there, and Bob didn't tell me this, but I can see it now. The southern dowager fumbling in her purse for smelling salts, while her daughter, who would have to be named Scarlet, runs for the lady's room in tears (for Wehle is a handsome devil, and he was single at the time), and the southern colonels push back from the oval, mahogany table, turning the color of Tabasco sauce and biting the ends off their Cuban cigars.

For Wehle had roamed the country and sketched every sharecropper hut he could find. This would be his theme. This would be his estate. A rough-hewn dog-trot with guest quarters that looked like sharecropper cabins.

Well I was a poor kid, and my folks never had the money nor time to take me out of Kansas, except to Arkansas to see some rag-tail kinfolk. So when I was "growed" it seemed I was bestowed God's providence, for I found myself wandering the silk and gold roads of the world.

I've walked the Hall of Mirrors in King Louis XIV's Versailles; hunted rabbits for Queen Elizabeth's corgies at her Scottish retreat, Balmoral; worked her Labs at Sandringham Castle; peeked into the Cathedrals of Assumption and Annunciation, and the Church of the Laying of Our Lady's Vestments as I strolled the Kremlin; had lunch in the Mexico City mayor's palatial garden. It goes on and on. I was quite a walker. I had a backpack. And God grew even more generous, and the world grew small.

But my point here is, in all the world there is no more charming, comfortable, and gracious complex than Wehle's beloved Midway holdings. And his fixins there—a fistful of tall grass tied and nailed to a bare door—are more fitting for that place than Michelangelo's renderings at the Sistine Chapel.

And I can't help but laugh—I'll just be driving down some dirt road going to get another dog story—and I'll laugh at the thought of those

A delight of Bob's, he excites pointer pups each morning with goose call and tidbits.

proper southern defenders of the faith, fainting and fuming at Bob Wehle's choice of brow-sweat architecture.

But back to Bob.

THE ULTIMATE GUN DOG

Wehle didn't set out to breed pointers that would win at Westminster or the National Bird Dog Championship at Ames plantation. No. He just wanted to raise a superlative gun dog for the average hunter. Something better than the world had ever seen before, something special. Something a shoe salesclerk, a bricklayer, a long-line trucker could take bird hunting and have a pleasant day with a pleasant dog. Something biddable. And quite frankly, folks, that's what we all want. But that ain't necessarily available for all gun dog breeds at this time. Not like it is for Wehle's English pointers.

Now this word biddable is very important. English pointers have had the reputation of being hard headed with carnal instincts that drove them to kill chickens and chase cats. Would you believe attack a cow? Wehle put a stop to that nonsense. His dogs are now famous for their trainability, their desire to please.

CONGENITALLY BROKE

Wehle says, "People don't understand . . . people who have these dogs . . . they call me and say, 'My dog is steady to wing and shot, and I didn't do anything with him. Did you break him before you sent him to me?' And that's the way it is, they're easy to manage. The breaking, which is a horrible word, *is in the breeding, not in the training.*

"And how did they get that way?" I ask.

Wehle is tall, he has an athletic build, and he has those rugged good looks of a seventy-year-old Sean Connery. He talks in merely a whisper—he is famous for this in dog training—as he says, "Today you saw nine puppies I was blowing the Canadian call for and handing out tidbits. That's the result of twenty-five puppies. Two of those have been sold. So that leaves seven. And I'll train those seven this summer and sort them out for all the things I like. Which is personality, intelligence, conformation, huntability. Maybe I'll end up with one out of that whole group. And he'll go into my full-time program. And that's what I do, year after year."

166

DEFECTS

"Once I had undershot in my kennels. The teeth would show above the bottom lip on some dogs. That's a recessive gene. Now I had a real good bitch Gypsy—who many said was the finest dog I've ever owned. I bred her to Snakefoot, one of the best males I've had in years. I expected something extra special. I got a male dog . . . Ohhh, what a dog. What could be better: a male from Gypsy by Snakefoot. And I'm walking the dog every day, and he's hunting and pointing birds and everything a puppy should be doing. He's independent, all class, high straight tail, and I was eight feet tall with this dog until one day he opened his mouth. He was undershot. He won't stay in my kennels.

"And this is what a man has to do to improve the breed. Regardless of how well he likes the dog, you have to bite the bullet. And this is what people are not doing. They're compromising and you can't do that.

"You see Jungle—he won the National Pheasant Championship three years running—was undershot . . . few people know that . . . but I lived with that for a long time. That's why I did the outcrossing I did with Red Water Rex."

(Remember Red Water Rex? Go back to chapter 2 and read where Hoyle Eaton whelps this pup and handgrooms him to the National Championship and the Field Trial Hall of Fame. After the many years that I've chronicled gun dogs, I'm no longer surprised to find great names circulating around and around and *ringing like the Olympic symbol through each other.* Red Water Rex became a foundation sire for Bob Wehle and was instrumental in making his English pointer kennels what they are. Greatness usually walks with greatness.)

Wehle says that after he went to Red Water Rex, "I finally got undershot out of my kennels. But it's a recessive gene. It will come back . . . very rarely. But it has to show up on this superlative pup."

Wehle's disappointment with undershot is not necessarily cosmetic. An undershot bitch can rupture a dog's naval when she tries to chew apart the umbilical cord. The solution is for the breeder to wait for the births, day after hour after minute. And sever the cord when each pup appears. That's not a whole lot of fun—I've done it.

GUN DOG BREEDING IS COMPLICATED

Wehle starts to get to the meat of breeding and genetics when he says,

"Breeding for one or two qualities is a relatively simple thing. Take the color phases of mink, they can do miraculous things with that. But with a bird dog you're breeding for a multitude of traits. There are so many X's in the equation, it gets so complex.

"Like a bench show . . . if you're breeding for conformation it is relatively simple. But not for a gun dog, a working dog. With a gun dog you're breeding for conformation, but you're also breeding for personality qualities. For example, you don't want a dog that trails [one that follows another dog while hunting]. You don't want a dog that's pugnacious. You don't want a dog that's lazy.

"You want a dog that has tenacity, that has a pointing instinct. And when you get one trait, you lose another you had." (Go back to the last chapter. Remember what I said about curing faults: Cure one, you get another. Same with breeding. So improvement is a slow, long progress.)

Wehle laughs now and says, "Seems like you can't ever get all the coons up the same tree."

LESSONS FROM DAIRY CATTLE

It is dark now, and Wehle's whispers hang in the air. I think for a moment and start to ask—but Wehle says, "Take dairy cattle [he bred a national butterfat Holstein champion]. Did I ever tell you about Professor Washburn at Cornell University at Ithaca? He indexed variables—you know they keep track of everything with a Holstein. So far as mother-daughter comparisons. How is their fat, their butterfat, how is their milk, percentage of butterfat, lactation period, and on and on.

"Well it was discovered young bulls produce the best Holsteins for all the things they check for. So I've been doing that. Breeding very young males. I bred Blaze when he was nine and one-half months old and got a pup that would knock you're eyes out. I bred Marksman when he was thirteen months old and got Jungle, and I bred Jungle when he was twelve months old and got Huckleberry. So all the time now I'm using very young sires."

THE START OF TRAINING

"The bottom line with an Elhew pointer is he's so easy to train because he wants to please. My dogs in the kennel don't bark because they want

A strong believer in roading for conditioning, Bob works pointer before horse.

to please me. I was never rough on them to accomplish that. Just my voice.

"You train with the tone of your voice, your mannerisms, your expression. I believe a dog knows when you're smiling. Certainly they know the inflection in your voice. And whenever I see a dog experiencing something pleasurable [recall Gary Ruppel's whistle trilling every time something pleasurable happens to a pup] I try to add my voice to that, so they will relate pleasantness with me and my voice. They relate to that. By the same token, if they do something bad I'll holler 'no' at them in a hoarse, corrective tone, and they seem to understand that. They understand they've hurt my feelings.

"Everything that the wolves do has a meaning. The way they carry their tail, the way they approach each other, their noses, and it's pretty much the same with dogs. If you watch a female with a litter of puppies . . . and just watch her manners . . . it takes you a couple of hours to sit there and watch. But she's talking to those pups half the time."

DOGS UNDERSTAND

"And those little puppies at a tender age seem to understand what she's saying. If they crowd her at the feed pan she tells them to stay back; it's her meal, not theirs. And they should understand.

"Now if they can understand her at that age, it just seems logical if you're a lot smarter than that dog is, you ought to be able to communicate with that dog when he's an adult.

"So I talk to my dogs on that basis. Believing they understand everything I say. And the proof's in the product: it pays off.

"Several dogs I've trained to be steady to wing and shot—it was done 99 percent voice. And there are so many trainers with so many dogs, they beat them with a whip, or bite their ear, or shock them with an electric collar. And that doesn't seem to be necessary at all.

"I don't know if my dogs are more receptive to that, but I believe they are: that is, training with intimacy instead of intimidation."

BEHAVIOR IS GENETIC

"You know behavior is genetic. Well you know it is; certain races of dairy cattle can be mean. There are strains of beef cattle, like Herefords. I've never seen a Hereford bull you couldn't walk up to and pat. Get a Holstein bull, and he'll kill you.

"Now I bred Snakefoot to Jubilee and got Bluenose. And if nothing happens, he's going to be a shiner. He's got incredible conformation, there's no way in the world I could chisel out a better dog than he is at this age. I might make a little improvement in his head, but his body is incredibly good. And his pointing . . . since he was a little dog he would point. And when he was a little dog I could take a stone and throw it in the grass and whistle, and he would come and point it. And he would hold that point with great intensity.

"Now that's inherent, and you've got to have that for a good dog. He's got great tenacity, and he has a great desire to see the other side of the county. Which I like. I want a horse in the bit . . . and Bluenose is in the bit.

"And that's what I'm looking for. And I'm looking for it at an early age. I don't like dogs that are puppies when they are eighteen months old. I want dogs to come into the world with business on their minds."

OUTSIDE STUDS

"Now I don't like to outcross for my studs. The reason being I've had a lot off dogs with problems that I had to correct or cover up. And they went ahead and won national championships, but still, I know that problem is in their blood, and I don't want to breed them. Zeus was a real nice dog in many ways, but he had a trailing instinct and that's genetic, and I broke him of it, and I won the National Amateur Championship with him. But he's not to produce.

"And when I go out to get a stud, it's like Zeus, I don't know if he's had a problem that they glossed over with training. [If] you breed outside, you don't know what that dog went through."

Bob stops talking. He has eaten and looks at my plate—I dawdle over my food for I'm always thinking. Never paying attention to the plate. Bob asks, "You didn't like the dinner?"

"Oh," I blurt, " . . . sure . . . sure . . . don't pay any attention to me, I was listening to you instead of eating."

He doesn't believe me, but he says nothing.

Then I ask, "Bob, you've had that problem with your colon, and now this bypass surgery—what was it, six bypasses? God I wish you life forever. I really do. I mean it. For I love you. And the world needs you. I need you. But what's going to happen to these dogs when you . . . you know?"

Bob smiles—he always smiles—and says, "I feel about my dogs like I feel about this place." He looks around the room. He does love it here. He says, "I don't want it clear cut. I don't want my dogs diluted and therefore the line destroyed. But they are going to be. Because nobody is going to go on. Except there will be . . . " And he says no more.

The room is silent and suddenly grows cold.

Bob looks at the table for a while and then says, "You know . . . [and now he smiles again] a hundred years from now and they're going to be looking for an Elhew pointer."

As I head for my slave quarters and that fluffed-mattress sleep, I turn back and see the lights go out in the dog-trot. I stand there under the tall pines and hear the night sounds. There are no mechanical sounds, no twentieth century sounds. It's miles to the road with its infernal machines.

And I recall Gary Ruppel telling us, "We couldn't train like this . . . all this sensitivity stuff . . . if it weren't for a new breed of dog." Bob Wehle

The sign that says it all: the finest gun dog kennels in the world. Bob carved and painted this one.

has just confirmed this. Tonight he told us his pups were born congenitally trained. They were "broke" in the womb.

"All you have to do to train an Elhew pup is talk to it," that's what Wehle said.

So without Wehle and others like him who are breeding a receptive pup—a pup who listens and wants to please—we could not be training the way we are. My standard would not exist with tenets such as "we train with our head, not our hand. We train with intimacy, not intimidation." Remember that. Remember Wehle. He changed the world of dogs.

A TESTIMONIAL

I think Wehle's contribution is best summed up by a letter I got from Mike Gould, April 6, 1993. He was guiding hunters in South Texas over a string of English pointers.

He writes, "I've got some bone-headed pointers and then the Elhews. No doubt about it, Wehle's pointers are intelligent. They're classy individuals, and most of them are natural retrievers, which is something that's always been a knock against English pointers.

"Elhews love to retrieve; they are affectionate; they're good house dogs, which is another minus against other English pointers.

"When I work an Elhew pointer I am marveled at how much they reflect Mr. Wehle's character and temperament. Of course he told me once, 'You breed dogs long enough and they get to acting like you.'

"Another thing. Elhews point birds from a great distance. And they get frustrated with the Texas dogs because they haven't smelled the covey, and the Elhews have to move past them.

"I hope I always have a few Elhew pointers around. Wehle's taken out most of the worry for me. He's made the gun dog trainer's job easy."

A couple of German shorthairs watch Web Parton shackle a training bird. (Photo by Nicole Poissant)

16

Web Parton

Web is a friend of mine. He is a fragile soul, an artist, a poet, a tender of bruised people and frightened beasts. He is that, and yet he is also a Hercules, for those who try to hunt with him are left leaning against poles gasping for breath. But with his dogs, who he calls sweety, or honey, or loved one, there is nothing, nothing at all under the sun, that he thinks as much of nor would do more for.

I'm hunting Gambel's quail with Web Parton near his home. As we walk along I break off long yucca stalks and lay them by, to pick up later. They will make great walking staffs.

The land is hot and dry. The dogs, two white-and-liver Llewellins, course before us. They are Web's dogs. They work as I've seen Llewellins work in England, where I recall a gamekeeper I hunted the day with exclaiming, "See, they run in a bow tie, and when they meet each other, they do not acknowledge the other, like two ladies passing who have never been formally introduced."

I look ahead for Parton. He has a slight build, with raven-black hair. A great mop of hair. And he smiles a lot, like he knows a joke on you. Parton is not tall, no taller than I am, actually. And yet, with no more than 150 pounds of ballast, he never carries less than eight canteens of water for his hunting dogs. That would be two gallons, and two gallons weigh sixteen pounds. Parton will do anything for a dog.

And I can't keep up with him. Nobody can keep up with him. And he's not showing off. That's just the way he goes. Straight out and straight up. Nothing deters him. Nothing detours him. He is the consummate outdoorsman.

When he was my neighbor, he would honk in my drive, and I would pile into his old faded-blue Nissan pickup, and we'd go up the Mogollon rim and dry hunt for elk, or antelope, or bear, or cougar. Web is a sustenance hunter and always has a pot on the stove for whatever he shot last. So he's forever scanning the tree limbs for squirrels, which he considers a delicacy.

But now he's bought himself some diggin's and built a training kennel in the old mining town of Oracle, Arizona, and I don't see him much anymore.

THE LETTER

So we write. Got a letter the other day, and in part of it Web says—but wait: He put a heading on the letter like it was an essay. It reads, "COVENANT OF PASSION." I told you he was a poet.

"I am in awe of our society's ability to spread information," he writes. "Yet I find we instruct with science and not art.

"Up until the 1950s, a dog had three years to become a bird dog. Now there are those, with a six-month-old puppy, looking for the thirty-day-wonder program. The poets among us might gently point out that the electric collar and the nuclear bomb were delivered to us about the same time and both work immediately.

"Modern gadgets can be a real asset in teaching a dog and communicating what he needs to do. They can save a pro trainer a lot of time. But they don't make a dog. The early dogs and trainers got by with a rope, a collar, and birds. Then, as now, what matters is there exists between the two a bond of trust and passion."

A REALITY WELL SAID

"Let me explain that.

"If a dog believes that you want the birds as much as he does. If he trusts that he will be treated with dignity and respect. If he knows his world to be a safe place even when he makes a mistake. He will live up to his genetic potential.

"On the other hand. When his world isn't safe, or he has no proxim-

Water is a constant need working in the Sonoran Desert.

ity to your passion because he passes his time isolated in a kennel run or worse, he is going to develop faults. Faults result from a breakdown of trust and a failure of passion."

COMMUNICATION

"There are many methods of dog training (communicating). No one method applies completely to each dog because each dog is unique. I have learned things from all of them. The knowledge is available to anyone ambitious enough to learn it. [Same thing Wehle said in the last chapter.] What is harder to find is an appreciation of the exchange that happens between dog and handler while the training is going on. The 'art' as opposed to the 'science.' There is mention of this as early as 1942, with a chapter entitled, 'Telepathic Communication Between Trainer and Dog,' in William F. Brown's book, *How to Train Hunting Dogs.* I personally feel that this is the level where training takes place."

DOG OWNERS

"A lot of dogs that are brought to me for training have already had something go wrong. When you love a dog, and you have a lot of personal feelings tangled up, and maybe a little guilt, it can be a difficult ball to unwind. The dog is entrusted to a professional trainer because his owner has lost faith in his ability to communicate with his dog.

"He doesn't know what to do. Some do nothing in lieu of doing something wrong. Others will do anything in lieu of doing nothing. Both approaches have a frantic quality to them. And neither does much to reestablish trust."

DOGS ARE SENSITIVE

"Dogs, like people, sense and respond to confidence. That is the atmosphere in which they learn best. I'm always very aware of what I'm feeling when I'm with a dog. It's not a matter of projecting what I want the dog to think I'm feeling. A dog knows what you are feeling.

"If it's been a bad day, then maybe force breaking isn't a good idea. Better to sit with each dog ten minutes on top of the force table and rub his belly and tell him what a fine bird dog he is going to make. That way, the session ends with both of you feeling much better, and the dog with happy memories of the force table. Experienced handlers learn that training is not about controlling the dog, instead it's about controlling oneself. [This was first stated by the immortal field trial trainer Clyde Morton, in *Field & Stream*. Clyde was having a rough day with a bird dog, and he dismounted his horse and went to a tree and slid down its trunk. He said to a niece who was there, "If I did one more thing to that dog I would destroy it. It's more necessary I control myself, than control the dog."]

"Once the training is done," continues Parton, "the ultimate goal of dog handling is not to have to. This can only happen with a dog that can think for himself, and who is not afraid."

I interrupt once again. What Parton defines here is a dog that has not been shock collar trained. A shock-trained dog usually cannot think for himself, and such a dog is often very frightened. He runs out of fear, not love. He hunts because he has to, not because he wants to. He is a mechanical dog—or an electronic dog—who has had all the self-will taken from him. The dog does not have what I demand a shooting dog have, and that is, "All the dog left in the dog." By that I mean, God gave us a dog who could do it all—without us. But man demanded he dominate. So he reduced the dog to an order taker.

That's not what I want. And that sure as hell ain't what the dog wants. Parton says a dog responds to the assurance of the handler. It's fact. And by the same token, a trainer feeds on the assurance of a dog. Give a trainer one of those self-confident, one-dog-in-a-million animals, and he'll be training in his darkened driveway by his kennel truck headlights.

RELATING TO A DOG

Now back to Parton who writes, "I use four ways of relating to a dog when we are training (communicating). In sequence, they are enthusiasm, disappointment, shaming, and intimidation. I lean very heavy on the first, and use disappointment sparingly. Shame is used as a last resort. There are some dogs who will ultimately require intimidation in brief doses. Intimidation by definition means the threat of pain. It can short circuit rampant uncontrollable passion when necessary. It can also combat stubborn willfulness.

"The fear of pain is what motivates here, not the infliction of it. If a trainer's repertoire consists solely of shaming and pain, the endeavor is

Time out for pulling cactus.

doomed. Pain is relative, and those who have experienced it at the hand of another will tell you that the sensation of feeling evaporates in short order and is overridden by anger and resentment. The soul grabs its passion and retreats inward. It will not appear again until it is certain of safety. That is a hard trust to re-establish."

THINKING IT OVER

So those were Web Parton's thoughts the day or night he sat and typed the letter. Hardly the missive you would have expected from an old-time dog trainer. Theirs was a time of hard-headed dogs, hard doin's, and heavy hands. Not that there weren't the sensitive among them. There surely was Clyde Morton. But think of what the old-timers put up with. Those trainers got in dogs that were escape artists, that grinned while they growled, that would go up your arm like it was an ear of corn.

We're getting in Wehle dogs now that are congenitally trained. Oh not all of them. But I still can't imagine anyone inflicting pain on a dog. Then again, if a pro's producing for wages, and the client must be satisfied. . . . What happens when the pro faces these circumstances?

Butch Goodwin in chapter 9 once had a dog that wouldn't respond to training. Butch tried every technique imaginable and a few that weren't.

Finally he phoned the owner and told him, "I can't get to this dog. He fights everything I do. You'll just have to come get him because I am not going to waste your money. He is untrainable."

The dog's owner replied, "Then I'll pick him up and have him put down."

"What?" cried Butch.

"I'll destroy him," repeated the owner.

So Butch relented and told the man, "Well, give me another week to see what I can do."

Poor Butch. And poor any dog trainer who is placed between this rock and a hard place. No trainer wants to see a dog destroyed. The trainer always feels it's his fault—never the dog's—that he can't get through. So anything like this would be a defeat for the trainer, and not much of a success for the dog.

So remember this: Trainers often times can't do what they want. They must defer to the owner.

AND I'M GOING TO TELL YOU SOMETHING ELSE

Web Parton speaks of pain. He writes, "The fear of pain is what motivates here, not the infliction of it." Then he writes, "Those who have experienced [pain] at the hand of another will tell you that the sensation of feeling evaporates in short order and is overridden by anger and resentment. The soul grabs its passion and retreats inward. It will not appear again until it is certain of safety. That is a hard trust to re-establish."

Have any of the trainers in this book known pain?

Could it be those who've been hurt don't want to hurt back? Especially to hurt a dog. The dog is defenseless, and some humane trainers may have been defenseless as youths or children. Does suffering make you sensitive? Caring? Gentle? What do you think? Would it make them conceive drills and techniques and equipment to replace pain. To moti-

Setter with brace of chukars takes break from morning's training. (Photo by Nicole Poissant)

vate and handle their dogs so praise becomes the drive, not the pain, the stick, the electric shock, the boot toe.

Many of us may have known pain. And we were helpless and we suffered and we remember. And we say we will not wish this upon a dog. Matter of fact, when I get all these dog books written, I want to work across this nation to elevate the dog's legal status. The dog is so gloriously and singularly sacred. Why do we consider him chattel? Why do we consider him beatable?

And what of the mind of beginning trainers? Do they become frustrated and lash out, and the dog is hurt, and he runs and cowers, and he never wants to meet this person again. And their whole relationship crumbles.

If so, that's why I've written this book. And why these trainers have helped me. Plus, it's why I've written all the books. To keep this from happening. And I write them because I care for the dog, not the human. The human can defend himself, the dog can't.

Somebody has got to be the dog's champion, and I'm one to raise his flag. Bob Wehle raised it long ago. And Web Parton, and Butch Goodwin, and Mike Gould, and Gary Ruppel, and everyone in this book.

That's why this is such an important book.

Not because I wrote it, but because of what it's written about.

Because it's written about the dog. And you know what a dog is? He's the symbol of faith between God and humans. God proved his love of humans by giving us the dog.

Buddy Smith calms pointer pup on point.

17

Buddy Smith

There're two more tenets to insert in our standard. First, a trainer must use land and the effects of nature to train his gun dogs. And second, there's not a problem that can't be solved with a bird.

When section hands brought the railroad west in the 1800s, they were intense and methodical: three strokes per nail, ten nails per rail, four hundred rails per mile. Mile after mile, day after day.

Buddy Smith of Collierville, Tennessee, trains gun dogs with the same steady deliberation. But there's another side to Buddy. He's bold with innovation. And what's that gotten him?

The first year I called on Buddy he'd just finished a good season in the National Bird Hunters Association's (NBHA) trials. That's where the dog runs and the handler walks: He ain't on horseback. Buddy posted seventy wins running shooting dogs, derbies, and puppies. This was an all-time high. And Buddy didn't post this record with two or three miracle dogs. No. He had a combination of ten pointers and setters. And he didn't stay on the road full-time to get the job done. He attended twenty-five NBHA trials during the year, averaging three placements a trial. That's unheard of.

With performance like this it's not surprising to learn Buddy has been named NBHA National Top Handler, runner-up Top Handler, runner-up National Top Handler Open Puppy, and Top Handler Open Puppy. And if you remember what we emphasized up front, that what should impress us here is a professional trainer excelling with puppies. I told you how well he handled pups was the ultimate test of a gun dog trainer. Well Buddy handles them well.

THE CALL-BACK PEN

The sixty-year-old, six-foot, dog trainer loads his dogs and me into his kennel truck and heads for his two-mile-distant training grounds. Buddy is a man who smiles a lot, an athletic-looking guy with Aqua Velva–blue eyes, with crow's feet at the corners from years of peering to horizons. Buddy parks near an inverted cotton wagon and asks, "Know what that is?"

"Sure, it's an old, rusted, beat-up cotton wagon someone's turned upside down."

"That's right. It makes the best bobwhite flight pen a dog trainer can have. Come on . . . I'll show you."

We start toward the wagon

"Just a minute," Buddy says, "I'll get a dog and show you sumpin'."
Buddy talks like that. He's country.

MAKING 'EM STEADY

A pointer dog, Buddy, and I enter the backdoor of the wagon to an explosion of bobwhite feathers and fine dust. The beating of the birds' wings is thunderous. "Whoa," says Buddy to the pointer, who has two thousand bobwhite dive-bombing his head. They even lift his ears with the force of their passing, but the dog stands like stone. Buddy goes forward to push all the would-be escapees back toward the dog and me. Here they come like shrapnel. "Whoa," says Buddy. The dog doesn't even blink. He stands solid as a storm cellar in a cyclone.

"And that," yells Buddy, "is how I make a dog steady. Just bring him in here enough times, and he'll honor the flight of a bird."

"I'd guess so," I say back. "One bird's sure not going to shake him after he's been buzz-bombed by two thousand."

Buddy walks back to me and says, "Bill, I like to start my puppy training from ten to twelve months. And I bring them in here with all these birds and a blank pistol. Maybe I shoot ten times when the birds are flying . . . all the time the pup's standing there watching those birds go by. I think it helps calm them . . . keeps them from breaking. Because when you're in a trial, and you go out to flush those birds . . . those liberated birds will fly right back by a dog. I've seen 'em walk under a dog's belly. But if you work them enough times at home like this . . . they are used to it in a trial. *A dog pretty well works a trial like he works at home.*"

"And you know that chain gang you're always writing about? [Re-

Pointer is taken into bird pen for pandemonium.

member Al Brenneman?] Well I use one here. I can put out twelve or fourteen dogs, and I flush these birds out of the cotton wagon and let the pups see them. Gets them excited, gets them knowing what a bird is and what a bird does."

THE TREE SHOOTER

Buddy grabs the dog's collar and leads him outside, turning to shut the door as he tells me, "I like to do things like that. Here . . . I'll show you. See that tree out there? Still got some green leaves on it? We'll just release a few birds and some of them will fly over there and then I'll work the dog into that tree and you see what happens."

Buddy reaches back to pull a rope that opens a door on the far end of the cotton wagon, and when enough birds have flown out, he releases the rope and the escape-door closes. Then he goes to his pickup for a shotgun and releases the pointer to work. "Whoa," Buddy murmurs as he walks forward to touch the dog's head, acknowledging work well done. Now Buddy walks in a great arc around the pointing dog and toward the tree when suddenly he stops and fires—not at any bird, but at the tree itself.

"See?" he yells. "The leaves . . . see the leaves? They're falling down on the dog. That's another way to steady them up. Shoot falling leaves over them. Even twigs and little branches."

The gun roars time and again, Boom, Boom, Boom, Boom, the leaves cascading and twirling down. The pointer may as well be sculpted of white marble. He seems not to be a part of this. This dog couldn't be moved off point with a tractor.

I walk over to Buddy and joke, "He's sure not gun-shy."

"That's right," Buddy replies, beaming, "and that's exactly what I do with gun-shy dogs . . . I keep them in that flight pen until they're broke, and then I come out here and shoot leaves all over 'em."

"Well I've never seen either technique used before," I tell him. "The closest I've come to it as a trainer having a gun-shy dog is to kennel him with live bobwhites while the dog's denied food until he catches birds to eat. That'll work," I tell him.

"Seems reasonable," the man says.

I'm joking when I tell him, "You must have an astronomical shell bill from shooting leaves off all your trees."

CONTINUALLY SHOOTING OVER DOGS

"Oh I do that even when there are no trees," reveals Buddy. "I shoot a lot over my dogs. When I get a young dog, I'll shoot while he's on point probably more than I do after the bird's flushed. That steadies them up quicker than anything I've found."

I want to sort this out so I ask, "You mean your dog's on point, and the bird's penned down, and you're shooting without flushing the bird?"

"Yep. And sometimes the bird will get up and fly off because of all the shooting, but if he does that's fine . . . that gives me a chance to correct my young dog if he breaks or creeps."

The man pets the pointer a moment then adds, "I don't have it today, but I usually wear a little bag 'round my waist, and I keep spare birds in there. So if a bird should fly away while the dog's on point, I've always got another one to throw down."

"You carry a sleeper, huh?"

"What do you mean by sleeper?"

"Well, let's say the bird flies away and the dog starts to break, but you get control of him. Now you can throw down a sleeper to convince the dog to always stay until you release him. Do it enough, and he'll always think there's a second bird to come up. That'll keep him both steady and rigid after the flush . . . looks good to the judges, plus it means you've got absolute control over him . . . you can relax at a trial not worrying all the time the dog's going to break."

"I know what you're saying," agrees Buddy. "I do that, and it works."

Now we're sitting in the pickup. A slight snow has started to swirl. Buddy says, "Those leaves I shot off . . . It encourages a dog to break. That's what you're trying to do when you're training at home, you try to make 'em make a mistake.

"If the dog breaks here, I can train. If he breaks at a trial, I'm finished. Here I can do something about him. At the trial all I can do is put him in the crate."

The wind wedges at the cracks trying to enter the pickup; I can hear it thump, and I can feel the truck sway.

A CASE OF SHELLS

Buddy laughs and says, "When an owner brings a dog to me . . . if he doesn't bring some shells, then later on after he sees the way I train, he brings lots of shells. That's the secret to getting a dog broke to wing and shot. Birds and shells. They don't cost, they pay."

HUNTING AND TRIALING

We take off as Buddy reveals something that seems constant among all great dog trainers. He says, "I like to both hunt my dogs and trial 'em. I like to load up my dogs and go to Texas. I can get into thirty or forty coveys a day in South Texas . . . kill a few. Just to sweeten up the dogs.

"If they point a covey I try to kill just one bird. Then I let them retrieve that bird. And if they point a single, I kill it and let 'em retrieve it. I'll hunt out there two or three days in a row and then bring 'em back, and they're a much better dog at a trial."

(Remember Bimbo West said he took the pup to South Texas, and "he came back a bird dog.")

Buddy yells over at me, over the roar of the truck engine, "You interested in whoaing pups?"

"Yea," I yell back. Since I'm thinking any man who can train a pup can train a dog, I want to see this man's technique.

FLAGGING

Essentially what Buddy does is position the pup to self-train. He explains, "Breaking dogs to wing and shot is something that I love. When I shoot a bunch of birds, I don't worry about my dog breaking; instead, my concentration is somewhere else. For example, when I walk back to that pup, I don't like to see him wiggle his tail. I like to see him hold that tail straight up and not do any crouching or flagging." The tails on Buddy's dogs look like antennas on cars. Straight up.

"I think what really tightens a dog up is yard work, and to do that *you've got to bond with the pup.* They want to please you, and when they are under control, they really listen to you. [Bonding? Pleasing you? Where have we heard that before?] When they listen real close, you have all of their attention. And when you have that, they aren't going to think about flagging."

I ask, "Then flagging is kind of an absent-mindedness?"

"Yes, and a lot of it is because of people holding a dog with a rope and trying to make him point. The rope won't allow a trainer to hold the dog's back end where that tail is. As a result the dog will start pulling on you, and then the back end gets loose and he starts flagging.

"Another way a rope gets you a flagging dog is that it causes you to walk forward to stand beside the dog and brace him. And when you do this, the dog gets to expecting you to brace him, and then he starts flagging.

"I don't want anybody standing beside my dogs bracing them. I just want the dog to brace himself. One on one. Plus, if the man moves, he could cause the dog to break. If the dog's alone, and he moves, that's the dog's mistake, and I know how to handle that. But don't ever blame a dog for breaking because a man prompted it. And you do prompt this whenever you walk close to or away from a dog on point.

THE WHOAING BARREL

"I start with yard work and get that whoa finished there before I ever bring the pup to the field. I do it with and without birds. One thing I do is use a barrel. Place a barrel in a cradle, or leave it flat on the ground, and build a scaffold over it. Put the pup there and rattle the barrel, make the dog think he's going to fall. He'll tighten up. And that's what steady to wing and shot is—becoming tight. Being on point.

Buddy shows pup beneath leafed-out tree. This is where he showers the pointing dog with falling leaves and twigs.

"Then I chain the dog to the scaffolding [an overhead beam] and present a tantalizing, flying, hobbled pigeon to him. Let that bird flap and jump. Let that dog be surprised and tempted. Rattle the barrel, pull on the dog's chain, let that pigeon keep up with what you call a feather dance. When I put the dog on the ground with the pigeon, the barrel's got him steady.

"You've also got to shoot a ton around your dog on point. When he's found a bird, walk up behind the dog—but leave some distance—and fire a .22 pistol several times. Walk around in front with a 20-gauge shotgun and shoot two to five times before you ever flush the bird. Use some live ammo and shoot twigs and leaves off trees above the dog."

(At this point it's important to break in with two key points. First, remember, we're positioning the dog to self-train. Second, live-shooting must, of necessity, be done in the country. And be careful! Don't shoot your dog, and don't have anyone else around when firing.)

Buddy continues, "Have everything that can spook the pup happen in training. Never let him get spooked during a hunt or at a trial."

"But what if the pup breaks with all that shooting?" I ask.

"I go back to yard work and correct him," Buddy tells me, as he stops

191

the truck. He exits and beckons me to follow him to a tall pole in the ground.

THE MAYPOLE

Buddy talks as he walks. "You put a section of one-inch PVC in the ground, then insert a ¾-inch piece of PVC that's fifteen to twenty feet long. At the top of this pole, attach seventy-five feet of nylon line. Tie a pigeon to the line. The pigeon will tire of flying and land. Whistle, tap your dog on the rump, and tell him to 'hie on.'

"The dog approaches from downwind and once again goes on point," Buddy tells me. Then he says, "You do all that firing, then go forward and lift the pigeon on the string. The dog watches it fly around and around in a 150-foot circle. Talk about both birdying him up and steadying him up! Then the bird lands and once again you tell the dog to relocate. This way you've got a constant flying bird that is always in view of the dog, and [the dog is] always waiting for a point."

HELPING A RANCHER

Back in the truck, we head for a neighbor's ranch. Buddy's trained there thirty years, and that's what each of us needs to do. Establish a relationship with someone who has land, so you have a place to run dogs. Pay the man back by looking for broken fences, knocked-down posts, abandoned calves, or trespassers.

Buddy puts two dogs down, and we follow them in the truck.

He says, "This is the ideal setup. You see the hedgerow and strip of grass beside it? Then next to the grass is a plowed-up field. Well, those dogs don't want to run in those jumbled clods, so they run instead on the level grass. The result? They're teaching themselves to run an edge. That's where they'll wind a bird. Ninety percent of all birds are found on the edge." (Smart, huh?)

PULLING A DRAG

"Another thing. I'll put a main-drive belt off a cottonpicker on one of those dogs. Either attach it to his collar or to his roading harness. That cotton belt makes a real good drag, and it doesn't scare the dogs like a chain would. You need about twelve feet to get the proper weight. At first, the dog will run with the belt dragging between his legs, but then

A flapping pigeon does not phase stone pointer on barrel.

he'll get wise and put his head to one side and get the belt off to the side.

"Now the reason for this dragging belt is that roading builds muscle, but running builds wind. Roading is where the dog's in a sled dog harness and he pulls against a tractor or car. But this way the dog is running free—dragging the belt. And a half hour with that belt is equal to an hour's running. It really builds the lungs and rib cage."

We follow the pups on the green grass for a half hour and then button it all up and head for Hardee's for biscuits and gravy. I'm thinking as we go, well, Buddy's shown us the value of birds and training with birds. Plus he's shown us how to use the land to teach the dogs to hunt productive cover.

And how would you do that otherwise? Oh you could walk on foot and keep hacking the dogs into the hedgerow. That's what most of us do. But Buddy's set up for mass production and time-saving. Nothing wrong with that, if he keeps a personal touch with the dogs. If he and the dogs are bonded, and they are, therefore, happy.

I remember another trainer who is a wizard using the land. I wonder if you'd like to spend some time with him? Let's go.

George Hickox and Llewellin setter stand before rushing Nova Scotia stream.

18

George Hickox

What do I mean by taking the effects of nature into training? Well, did you know you'll play Billy hell casting a swimming retriever into the wind? Or that the same dog running at angle up a hill will sour off downwards? Or that heavy cover will turn a dog. Or that dogs are very aware of place. And if a dog's hurt somewhere, he never wants to go there again. So let's see how Hickox handles the needs of a ruffed grouse dog. It'll be interesting.

A ruffed grouse dog must hunt quietly, in nearly impenetrable cover, and stop at the absolute edge of the bird's scent cone. Consequently, these three realities determine all his training.

I'm hunting Nova Scotia with George Hickox, an upland game guide who trains Llewellin setters and English springer spaniels. We have a delightful hunt for four reasons: there are tons of birds, few rural inhabitants (in one week we never met a hunter with a grouse dog) the country is pristine (no litter, for example), and the scenery is incomparable.

About nine o'clock in the morning, Hickox releases a black-ticked Llewellin, and we saunter down a tote road through a kaleidoscope of late foliage with that dull patina of heirloom silver. Hickox says, "You're a Lab man, aren't you?" I tell him, "I train and hunt all gun dogs." "Well," he says, "Ever hear of the guy who named his Lab 'Herpes'?" "No," I tell him. He laughs and says, "The dog wouldn't heel."

Thus I am introduced to a week of banter and bruising cover, bad jokes, a bevy of birds, and beautiful dog work.

Here's how Hickox trains these grouse dogs.

MOWED ROWS

"The important part of my early training is patterning work," says Hickox, a neat, fortyish, hard-working guy with nonstop talk. He's transplanted here from New England, having married a Canadian gal. "My field is cut in rows," he tells me. Now this is important. "They are horizontal . . . you imagine I'm walking north to south, these rows are cut east to west. What I do is take a brush hog and cut a five-foot swath and miss the next row. There's 150 rows: that's 750 feet.

"Now a young dog runs the low rows, as I do almost spaniel-like training in the early patterning for a pointing dog. Because I'm not looking for a wide-open country dog. I'm looking for a dog that's going to stay relatively close. And I don't like to do that with pressure. I like to do that with ingrained habit."

Another trainer who uses the land to train instead of blind force.

BREAKING COVER

"I plant a bird down in a high row to left or right, and then I have to encourage the pup to leave the mowed lane and break cover. But Wow! When he learns there's birds in that tall stuff, he starts hunting. And this is most important: The dog breaks cover because he winds the bird. Any gun dog must learn to use the wind. And cover can be no concern to a grouse dog.

"Now before that . . . say when the pup is seven weeks old . . . I have Johnny houses of quail all around the puppy kennel [recall pens like Buddy Smith's cotton wagon]. So hundreds of birds are let go. Plus, these birds are in the alders—the primary place the pup will later hunt ruffed grouse.

"So now the pup is having fun, hunting, flushing, chasing, but most important: learning to use his nose."

RELEASED BIRDS

"These released birds guarantee the pup instant success [excellent, because a pup has a short attention span]. Then we go to the row-training for now the pup knows what a bird is.

"I don't like the concept of whistle, whistle, and telling the dog, 'By Gosh I told you to do this or that.' So I feel if these nearby birds establish

The nondrinking author was billeted in this distillery for his Nova Scotia ruffed grouse hunt.

success for the puppy, then when he's a dog he'll be successful in finding wild birds.

"The dog has a natural ability to hunt, that's genetics. But to learn to hunt effectively, and that's what it is, it's learning—the young dogs with the packs, the wolves, those dogs are going out with their elders and they learn how to hunt—they learn how to position themselves with the wind so they can eat." (That's what flat-coat specialist Ken Osborn called birdcraft.)

WHISTLE TRAINING

"Now while wind-patterning on the high-low rows, the pups are dragging a check cord. Okay, at eight to ten months they get a long check cord, and I introduce the whistle with a 'beep, beep.' That beep, beep is a casting out, plus a hard turn afield. Primarily I'm going to use a roll whistle . . . a soft, continuous trill. As long as I keep trilling, the dog is going to come back. Imagine a kite string. The roll whistle keeps that dog at the edge of bell range [grouse dogs wear a bell on their collar], and it also lets the dog know where the hunter is in thick cover.

"Then with the check cord portion we twitch the cord, beep, beep. Twitch, beep, beep. So now we've got a dog that knows how to hunt, give to the lead, and use the wind to find a bird. What we don't have is a staunch dog.

"I'm looking at a grouse and woodcock dog, and I can't have the dog creeping. What I want is a dog that as soon as he gets a wisp of scent, he stops. Even if he's not identified exactly where the bird is. Grouse aren't always going to be the tightest sitting birds in the world. Woodcock will be, you can make a lot of mistakes on woodcock that you can't make on grouse.

"All right, now we plant a bird. The dog smells it. And I walk up the check cord and hold his collar. A helper makes a lot of hoopla to excite the dog, to make him crazy over birds. Then later I can use an electronic bird launcher."

STOPPING AT THE EDGE OF THE SCENT CONE

"Now this is important. Soon as that dog indicates with just a little turn of his head where he's saying, 'Whoops, I've smelled something here,' I stop him with the cord, with no talk, for whoa is a yard-training thing, not a bird-training thing.

"The reason for that is I don't want that dog to ever think he's done something wrong around a bird.

"Now to the electronic bird launcher. Once that dog points on his own I'm going to fire that bird out of the electronic sling the second the dog takes a step. The game is over when he takes that step. He can't get any closer—that's what I'm teaching him. What the grouse dog will do is this. He'll be saying, 'I don't have that bird identified, so I'm going to take a step forward.' But in training, boom, that bird is out of there. Because, in hunting when the dog takes a step forward, boom, that grouse may be out of there and you won't get a shot.

"So the procedure is, the dog goes on point, period. Then when I get to him in the field, if he doesn't know where the bird is, I can release him with a click of my cheek. The point is, I release the dog—he never releases himself. There can absolutely not be any creeping on a ruffed grouse.

BE QUIET

"Now something else. This grouse is a spooky bird, so everything must be hospital-quiet. No loud whistle, no human voice, no dog commands. Consequently, you don't have the opportunity to say, 'Whoa, whoa, whoa.' Which means that grouse dog has to be rock steady before you ever take him to field. . . . In training your foundation [this] must be absolutely solid. If you don't demand excellence . . . you won't get excellence."

So that's the way George Hickox talks. It is nonstop and forever. Finally, I do get a word in to ask, "How do you get the dog to honor the edge of the scent cone?" Whew, I made it.

"I use two slip leads tied together," says Hickox, "and I've got one around the dog's haunch and another around his neck. What it looks like is straps on a suitcase. I can actually pick the dog up and walk him away."

THE CANINE SUITCASE

"I want that haunch-strap to keep the dog from sitting on point. You've always got to work against that with a setter. So I've got these two straps in hand and walk the dog along and say, 'Whoa,' and if he starts to take a step, I literally pick the dog up. There's nothing about it being a bad guy on my part. It's just repetition, over and over. And the dog learns it. When I but whistle whoa in the grouse field, the dog turns to stone."

Hickox takes a left oblique to look for his dog in cover that's—well, let's put it this way: If you can't take a good swipe of briar in the face, don't take up grouse hunting. If ruffed grouse were my holy grail, I'd go to the woods in the summer with a chain saw and cut paths. Honest, folks, you can't get a tank through this stuff.

When Hickox returns with his dog I tell him, "Let's go hunt the abandoned apple orchards." The cover will be wild grass and wait-a-bit vines you can avoid.

And we try that with no luck. You see, summer stayed late in Nova Scotia this year, so the apples didn't fall and ferment. Grouse don't want to eat a hard apple. Plus, now the rains have come, and the grouse are holed-up in the spruce trees. No upland game bird wants to get wet.

Hickox guides for pheasant as well as grouse. English springer spaniel hups to flush.

DON'T OVERHANDLE

Hickox walks me toward another copse when he says, "It's important in training to remember the dog knows where the hunter is [even though] you've each lost eye contact with the other. So again we come back to the foundation portion. Which means this: If you don't have eye contact, the dog must learn to use his own head. And that means he always stays within bell range and always hunts into the wind.

"Most guys try to overhandle their dog and pretty soon the dog is tuning them out—and the handler has forced that. So in the grouse woods everything must be low-key and easy going. Frankly, that makes a great hunt."

And so it does, and so it did.

But what's important to you and me is realizing how Hickox used those series of high- and low-cover rows to teach his pups to break cover. Excellent. A real use of this man's head. And that's what we have with

200

today's training. Thinking ahead, creating unique uses of nature that direct the dog, instead of a handler hacking at him from behind with loud voice and glaring face. Or worse yet, a shock collar.

And folks, that's what this book and this new humane movement is all about. Being bright enough to train a dog without hurting it. By psyching it, and tricking it, and motivating it, and keeping it happy all the while you're doing it.

Domination in gun dog training is dead.

And the dog trainers who still use it are soon going to be out of business.

If Bud Daniels had money, he could have been a banker. Instead he had birds, so he trained dogs.

19

Bud Daniels

We've met the practitioners, now let's relax and include a humorist. A guy on the firing line every day guiding hunters. A guy who's got to keep the banter going as well as the dogs. Meet Bud Daniels who has more than a little to say about today's dogs and today's men.

Bud Daniels is one part gun dog trainer and one part grassroots philosopher. Not only is his job to train up gun dogs you can shoot over, but to entertain you while you're doing it.

This six-foot-two-inch, 226-pound combination Arkansas native and Texas migrant (he trains in Arkansas during the hot summer months and hunts bobwhite in South Texas during bird season) says of himself, "I'm like a mule. I have no pride of ancestry and no hope for posterity." You got to be dirt folk to recall mules can't reproduce.

And that's the way Daniels carries on, saying such things as, "Never hire a man who wears a straw hat or smokes a pipe . . . he's forever chasing that damned hat or packing that damned pipe." His wisdom is deep and rustic—always with a touch of humor—and he makes a master hunting host. Here's how he works.

THE BIRD DOG BUSINESS

He can be an independent contractor, booking his own hunts, catch as catch can. Or he can contract with a business that wants to entertain customers, award employees, and develop new clients. Such firms pay for the lease, buy the truck, furnish the noon meal, and do whatever else they fancy. Then Bud shows up at the lease gate at sunrise, waits for the sports, and when they arrive, he takes them hunting over at least twelve bird dogs he'll carry at all times so there'll always be a fresh brace down.

"My job," he says, "is to accommodate the customer, and I put down sure'nuf-trained bird dogs, conditioned, field- and bird-wise, with plenty of bottom in them to get the job done. You know in South Texas if the scenting conditions are poor, then that means they've picked up. We don't have a wind, we don't have a breeze, we've got a southeastern drift, and we develop dogs that can work on that paucity of help."

WE'VE GOT BIRDS

"But we've got the birds. Why I've moved as many as thirty-seven coveys of bobwhite in one afternoon. The other day we stopped by a windmill for lunch. And while they were putting the trash in tote sacks, I let two dogs loose. We never left that windmill until we got into eight coveys. And when I say we ran into thirty-seven coveys you've got to realize, we were delayed mightily by the gunners getting off and back on the hunting truck."

DOGS ARE BETTER THAN EVER

Daniels, who played pulling guard at Arkansas in a single wing formation, and surprisingly has a degree in forestry (I look around the area for a tree), starts talking about people today and their gun dogs. He says, *"Dogs are better than they've ever been,* it's people who aren't what they used to be. Most dogs have been bred now to the point of where they have all of the best in inherent qualities.

"But most people who own these high-bred dogs usually have a job somewhere and can only train or bird hunt on a weekend. Now these dogs are taken care of feed-wise, medically; they're in excellent shape as far as everything but being conditioned, and the guy lets the dog loose on a weekend, and by Sunday night he's not even started to get the edge off."

THE OLD-TIME DOG

"Used to be, when the dogs stayed up under the house and you walked out with your shotgun and they heard the bolt fly to and they'd come out from under there ready to go and it was over the fence at a real leisurely gate, and they had finding birds on their minds instead of seeing what was on the other side of that ridge . . . because they had already seen what was on the other side of that ridge.

"And we say those old-time dogs were better bird dogs. They weren't.

[They weren't better bird dogs, they were better "natural"-trained bird dogs.] We're just not the people that we used to be because our lives are geared different. Nobody has the chance to live on the land and get out to the fields each day. And that's what a gun dog needs."

THERE'S NOTHIN' TO BREAKING A BIRD DOG

"Shucks there ain't nothing to breaking a bird dog. South Texas is such a wonderful place because you can sit there on that hunting truck and that dog can go through covey after covey after covey and make all his mistakes and keep making them over and over and you know just as soon as he's cleared that one there's another one over there just a few steps. And that's not just with one dog, that may be with four or five down and that running lets them get all those mistakes out of their system." (Remember, you can't make a bird dog without a bird.)

TAKES BIRDS TO BREAK A PUPPY

"It's not like Arkansas where I come from where we've gone from a small subsistence farming–patch economy to one that's oriented toward large ownership and primarily timber. We still have a lot of birds in the woods . . . more than you'd probably think and a lot more than you'll probably see. But to try and break a puppy up there where you can't see him at all times, and you only hear a whir and see a blur . . . and you scream, 'Where did he go?' 'Did the puppy flush him?' 'I don't know?' 'Well catch him and whip him anyway. . . .'"

MY HOME STATE: KANSAS

"And it may be until tomorrow afternoon before you see another covey of birds. We'll take two years to break a young dog up there and in less than sixty days down here with a dog that's mature enough to be ready to break, and if he's good . . . in two months time . . . you can do more with him than in two years time anywhere else, except Kansas.

"But even there ownership patterns restrict what you are able to do and what you want to do. But down here it is so easy. You're sitting on that truck most of the time. And you see forever and ever. Dogs learn to handle because they need a drink of water as much anything else. And they learn to come to the truck. And you can do your culling on a lot different basis down here. The first thing you look for in a dog in South

Bud trains this way only for author's photo session. "The way to make a bird dog," says Bud, "is to put him on wild birds."

Texas that's ready to break is bottom. That is, if he's got the go, he can't help but intercept birds. But in Arkansas and Kansas a dog has to learn where birds live. He's got to learn to go to the edges. He can run to the middle of some of those places up there in that rolling prairie and turn around and look at you, like, 'what am I doing here?'

"Now a dog broke in Arkansas and brought to Texas does a good job because the birds are everywhere, and he doesn't have to find them. There are edges down here, but they are not as clearly defined. But at the same time, a dog broke in Texas and taken to Arkansas still has to learn. Because he's got to learn to go to the edges; he's got to learn all about heavy cover. He'll go over, and he'll start jumping high and looking at you, like, 'how much farther do we have to go before we start to hunt?'

"And that is one of the differences. But back to what I wanted to emphasize. You don't have to do a lot of yelling and hacking down here to train a dog. That dog knows where you are, and you know where he is, and you keep pushing . . . the one that does not turn into a bird dog is the exception.

"*And you don't have to beat him into it* . . . they finally figure out if they don't move on point the birds won't move. In a lot of cases. But if they do move, the birds are going to move. And when you start shooting birds in front of them, and they get their mouth on a bird with that gun going off, you've got it made."

We're yard training dogs today, check cording them into a hobbled pigeon's scent cone. This is not the way Bud trains. He's all for getting dogs into natural birds. But he's consented to help me test something, and we're also taking lots of pictures. Finally Bud says, "*You know it's birds that make a bird dog.* Like me. I was always meant to be a banker, but nobody got me into money. How could I be a banker with no money? *Same with these dogs. How can they be [bird dogs] with no birds?*"

THE OLD PULPWOOD BUSINESS

"And you don't worry about things," he says. "Years ago I was in the pulpwood business, and my whole living depended on ground conditions. And if it were raining, we were out of business; we couldn't get out of the woods. And I spent half of my time concerned about the wood job because it was wet weather, or winter, or something like that. I thought the perfect way to solve this is I'll plant me a big corn crop. That way if it's wet then I'll be glad for the corn, and if it's dry I'll be glad for the wood job.

"But the outcome was I ruined what half-time had. When it was wet, I worried about the wood job, and when it was dry, I worried about the damned corn. So do your best with your dog and don't worry about it. But I do advise you to get him into tons and tons of wild birds."

Bud brings a dog into the bird's scent cone and says over to me, "And don't pay too much attention to so-called 'experts.' A man went to the doctor the other day and told him his left leg hurt. The doctor laughed and said, 'Why that's just old age.' The patient snapped back, 'Like hell it is . . . my other leg's the same age, and it don't hurt.'"

I LIKE DOGS

Now Bud walks up to me and says, "I like dogs. They respond to the care that I give them, they are faithful. I like them because every time I go to get them, they do what they are supposed to do. Not a one of them ever said 'I don't want to go.' And when I get through with them and put them away, not a one of them says, 'Where you going when you leave here?' And when I get back there isn't a one of the them that asks, 'Where you been?'"

WHAT DOES A BIRD DOG SMELL?

I'm laughing as I ask Bud, "There's a theory that dogs smell quail's breath. That's what they're pointing. Any ideas on that?"

"Yea . . . I don't believe it. What I do believe is bird dogs smell bob-white droppings. I guarantee you get a covey rise or a couple of birds get up out there that a dog's got pointed, and you watch them . . . they'll go fifty, sixty yards, and they'll dump in the air. You've seen 'em. Now the dog hasn't seen that, okay? But when he crosses that track where those droppings fell he'll shut down just a second then pick up and go on.

"If birds are in one place and have been there for any period . . . three or four minutes . . . they're easily detected by the dog. But a bird we used to call 'airwashed,' he just went in—we saw him go in—and there's enough cover to hold him . . . the dog goes in and can't smell him for anything. And finally we kick the bird up, and the dog hasn't smelled him, and we say 'the dog is no good . . . he has no nose.' I'll say there wasn't something there for him to smell. I say there were no droppings for him to scent in on."

The day is done and as I'm leaving, Bud yells at me, "We ought to farm like in Biblical times . . . the vow required you leave so much for the gleaners, the edges had to be left, and the poor were allowed to come into the field after the wealthy had gathered the crops they were allowed to gather. That's what I think it ought to go back to instead of farming fence-row to fence-row with quail carrying their lunch across a lot of these fields."

I wave at him, climb into my car, and pull out. A day with Bud Daniels is a treat. No wonder he's become bobwhite's master host.

SO WHAT DID WE LEARN?

Lots. Bud once again emphasized we have a much better class of dogs. That these dogs are easily trained if you let them run wild amid tons of birds. And once again, Bud spoke of targets of opportunity for bird dogs, objectives, if you will. That is, how they must hunt an edge, they must know their territory, and they must know what their quarry is doing each hour of the day.

Bud also chastises the modern American male for working for pay. For not living with, and on, the land. Not having that opportunity to take his bird dog with him to the filling station, the grain elevator, the swimming hole, the local checker parlor. And that's a fact I've lamented in many books.

The result is: The dog can only be a part-time performer.

Bud also shows us you can train a dog to hunt birds with just birds. No drills, no equipment, no repetition, no contact, and really no association with the handler. For years that's the way it was done—and then man left the land.

Bud also shows us how natural features affect dog training. He illustrated how it was nearly impossible to train a bird dog in that dense cover of Arkansas. He opined Kansas had some value, and I agree, for that's where I sprung from. That's where I learned. But he didn't mention the best feature about Kansas. Kansas has birds because Kansas has feed. Birds will never abandon their grocery store if it's kept stocked.

Bud has a lot to say and says it well. He has fun being a dog man and really, that's the way we all should behave. None of those long faces. None of that, "Damn, the dog blew the series." Who cares?

It ain't a ribbon that's important anyway. And really, it's not a bird. It's you and that dog. That's what's important. That's what's magic.

A young Reverend Walt Cline just starting with his English cockers.

20

Walt Cline

We've learned much in this book but possibly the most important revelation has been, "The breaking's in the breeding." For that reason I want you to meet the guy who saved the cocker spaniel in America. An unlikely, threadbare hero, he didn't have a dime to do it.

Everything's surprising in the story you're about to read. It involves the cocker spaniel, a dog named for it's adaptability at hunting woodcock. But the high plains of eastern Wyoming are a far cry from the woodcock's favored habitat of a bog-bordered creek with lush fern and dripping tree leaves.

But that's where this cocker story takes place.

And the man who saved the cocker is not some Anglophile wearing knee britches, a waxed coat, and tam. This guy would be hard-put to find among his possessions a blue-jean jacket that still had the elbows in it.

So down from the Rocky Mountains dips this monotonous high prairie, with it's heat-stroke summers and frozen-bone winters, where the wind blows with glee, the rain is driven to earth by eternal lightning, and the night sky shows starlight as dense as viewing a broad city from a high hill.

And here at Newcastle, Wyoming (Walt has since moved to Alliance, Nebraska), where green Burlington-Northern engines rumble by, hauling endless hoppers of coal—none of them more than forty feet from this front porch—I look at the toys scattered about the yard, and knock, knock, knock on the scuffed door.

HIGH NOON

The man appears. Ruffled. A wayward tuft of hair hanging over his forehead like Gary Cooper in *High Noon*. He is a big man, and he stands there looking at me with gentle timidity. In a slow and measured way he asks, "Are you Bill Tarrant?" Anyway I guess that's what he asks for the diesels are really whining.

The man opens the door, and I reach in to shake his hand. This is Walt Cline, thirty-four years old at the time. A small-town preacher, poor as a church mouse, totally without sense of self, nearly a zealot in his love for dogs and Christ.

Walt's been a bird hunter since he was a fourteen-year-old farm boy. He's risked bread and bed to assemble the seven cockers that run through our legs after we leave the house and head for a pond.

ETERNAL SIGNIFICANCE

Walt says, "I wanted to be a game biologist, or something out in the fields. But somewhere along the line I heard an inner voice tell me there was more eternal significance in directing a man's soul to God than in saving another canvasback duck. Yet," he grins, "I've always kept the duck in mind."

AMERICAN COCKER SPANIELS

He arches a training dummy high over the water, and all seven cockers leap hearty as frogs and pump vigorously for the fetch. Walt says, "I tried to do it with ACSs. And I can be—"

"What," I ask. "You tried to do what with what?"

"Oh," answers Walt, "ACS . . . that is our way of saying American Cocker Spaniels. ECS stands for English Cocker Spaniels. Anyway, I tried to make gun dogs out of ACSs . . . and it can be done. But what a chore. Take Dolly out there, she's American bred. Oh she'll hunt . . . you can always entice her with a bird. But field-bred cockers are more intense, have a stronger natural retrieving instinct. And they just tend to do more things naturally.

"American show-bred cockers have a latent ability that can be developed. To get Dolly, for example, to hold a bird I'd stand her on the table and put a bird in her mouth and praise her for holding it. It took hours and hours.

Five wet cockers beg Walt for one more water retrieve.

"And when I took her afield, everything had to be immediately successful, or she'd lose interest."

ENGLISH COCKER SPANIELS

"But the ECSs jump out of the crate hunting . . . and they don't even know what they're looking for. Plus their instincts seem to intensify as they grow older."

Walt keeps talking and the pack swims back toward us, trying to drown the one with the training bumper. They leap over each other, go under, cavort, and yes, laugh.

What Walt says about cockers is worth our attention. He's paid his dues, having told me, "My take-home pay was $160 a week, but I had to have this ECS and the price was $750. He was supposed to be started. And he was worth it to me, because I had a full-litter brother of his that got killed, and I knew what the blood could do. *So I sold all but two of my shotguns and an old hunting pickup I had and bought the pup.*"

On another day when we were working the cockers, Walt confided,

"My first two ECS imports came in the same crate and cost me $1,269, including air freight."

THE LAWN ORNAMENT

But he explained the sacrifice, saying, "Here I saw this magnificent little gun dog going down the tube . . . becoming a lawn ornament, if you know what I mean. And I was saying, 'Somebody has to do something. Someone has to save the blood.' But then I remembered that's what I'm always telling my congregation. When something has to be done, do it yourself. Don't stand there saying, 'Why doesn't somebody do something?'"

CONFORMATION

The cockers are leaping about us now and shaking water and running to dry their faces by rubbing them sideways against the sparse grass. Walt points out, "*Show-bred dogs have characteristics that are a hindrance to field work.* Look at Dolly. Her coat is not suitable for the field. I can show you pictures of her with snowballs all bound up under her legs. And I was picking her up, breaking the snowballs off and it was terrible . . . the mallards were flying and there I was messing with a dog.

"But Whisp and Daley, my two English imports, didn't have more than a couple of little balls . . . those in places where it wouldn't hinder them. Turn Dolly over and look under her armpits . . . there's lots of hair there that matts, and it has to be trimmed out. But Daley, in those places where he rubs, there's no hair. And just as important there's no hair in his ears.

"The show cocker's ears set real low on the head, and they are so long they've become tubelike. This shape and the excess hair encourages debris to work up and enter the ear canal. This is especially bad since the cocker may be working below seed level in the field. But the field-bred cocker has his ears set up on his head, the ear is flat . . . not like a tube . . . and there's no hair on the inside to transport debris.

"Plus the show cocker's feet are too hairy. Always [need] to be trimmed. Not with the field bred. Also, texture of the hair is different; the field-bred cockers hair doesn't collect debris.

"But the big advantage of ECSs in general over American cockers is their eyes are set deeper in the head. Americans have gone for Bambi eyes. There's consequently more eye surface to collect junk. The dogs are pop-eyed, which means the eyes can easily be contaminated or injured in the field while hunting.

"So tight eyes, good field coat, naked ears, ear conformation that mitigates against debris entry—these are the desirable characteristics of the ECS. But the most important thing is their intensity, their desire. And they have the biddability to learn, or else you'd just have a sky rocket. Plus, there's more fun to an ECS if you do it in the water. They just make great retrievers. And they'll retrieve all day.

"There seems to be less consistency in size in field dogs than in show dogs," explains Walt, "so when you buy a show dog you get uniformity in conformation and a great disparity in ability. You don't know what you're going to get. In the field-bred dog you've got uniformity of ability and instinct, and some disparity in conformation. A small bitch could weigh only twenty pounds, field-fit. Could be as short as fourteen inches at the withers. That's absolutely tiny. A large male could be eighteen inches tall and weigh forty pounds. And that's solid muscle.

"But again . . . apart from all that . . . the field-bred cockers have great quartering, driving, hunting, and birdiness instincts the show bred won't necessarily have."

THE VEST POCKET RETRIEVER

We've moved on to brush and stubble that grows north of the pond. The cockers are racing after a released pigeon, but Walt keeps a couple of birds in his pockets to roll out before him in case the pack runs beyond gun range. This will pull them back.

He says, "They can fetch anything. A sage chicken weighs six pounds. They'll bring that to you. And a goose! What more could you want? That's what I have to hunt here in Wyoming: sage chicken, pheasant, waterfowl. They'll do it all. Not only that, they're probably the best all-around gun dog for all the different birds we have in America. They'll hunt bobwhite for you. But it's considered a fault if they point . . . they're supposed to give you a quick flush. Still, I've sold some pups to guys who are trying to make them into pointers."

A seasoned Walt Cline finding love as much as ever in the caress of a cocker. (Photo by David Williams)

VERSATILITY

"It's versatility . . . that's what I like," declares Walt. "If you're hunting pheasant and jump a mallard off a pond dam . . . the English bred is going to fetch it for you. Even rabbits. And they'll take briar, they'll break ice, they'll suffer corn stubble. Matter of fact, if you don't watch them, they'll kill themselves getting a bird.

"Dolly jumped off a cliff after sage chicken. Swift jumped off a cliff after a pheasant and got a herniated disk. That shows eagerness, doesn't it?"

There's no need my saying yes, or anything else. Walt's missionizing now. He's got the dog pulpit, and he's giving his summation.

"Where I see the cocker," he says, "is where the fellow is not able to run with the pointers anymore: They're just too hot and too hardheaded for the fellow who lives in town, the apartment dweller. My whole kennel of cockers doesn't eat what two of my pointers used to eat. A guy who does a variety of things needs a cocker . . . he doesn't know what he'll be hunting next, and the *cocker doesn't care.*"

THE KIDS DOG

"And your kids—you just can't go wrong with an English cocker if you love them a little. They thrive on it . . . and give it back. A pointer or a Chesie could drive a kid nuts. But the cocker won't knock the baby over, or tail-whip the knickknacks off the end table. The cocker is for the family man, the guy who doesn't get out every day to hunt. But then, he's for the young guy, too, the kid who hunts every day."

The cockers keep hunting as Walt keeps talking. I like this preacher. I like his dogs. I like anyone who moves hell and high water to save a dog—or his fellow human.

REVIEW

So again our resolve is buttressed to include only the best of the best in sire and dam when picking a pup.

This is not to say some indiscriminate backyard mating might not produce a winner: it has, and it will. But the certainty is not there.

Whereas, to go with an established breeder, your chances of getting a rip-snorter is enhanced.

You just can't drive a '29 Ford in the Grand Prix. And you can't take a sorry dog and win the national or forge a legend as the best hunting dog who ever lived.

THE BENCH PEOPLE

Also, our visit with Walt underlines the harm done by bench fanciers when they get their hands on gun dogs. They too often render them unfit for the field. That's why you should never buy pups from a bench litter and hope to go hunting. Again, the exception does happen. But why play the odds?

And we see this bench destruction with so many of our prized hunting dogs. Take the golden retriever. Jim Charlton tells us they're getting their muzzles so short they can't even pick up a goose. He also tells us they're going for the lightest color they can breed, turning them out platinum blonde if they can.

I don't know why bench people are this way. So dysfunctional. What differences does it make what color a dog is? If I had one with a green coat, five legs, and two heads—but he could outhunt any dog alive—he'd share my bed and breakfast.

We saw this color thing with a brown Lab. When I used to spend so much time in the British Isles, I came upon a lady north of Scotland—out on an island—who was breeding white Labradors.

ODD DOG: ODD COLOR

I suppose it goes back to this. If a guy or gal can't train a dog, then at least they can say, "He's an odd color." They can say, "He's different." For the same reason these punk kids dye their hair blue, I guess. They have no skills to do anything of value—but they're different.

I want all my dog differences to mean more birds in the pot.

Plus, we remember Bob Sprouse's review of the Irish setter, and in this case the dog was rendered so unfit, the Irish supporters had to go to Bill Brown (he was quoted by Web Parton), editor of *The American Field* and head of the Field Dog Stud Book, to authorize an outcross to an English setter. Thus we have the red setter.

GREAT BRITAIN

We find another man, Walt Cline, sacrificing to bring a dog in from England. It was Great Britain who gave us our field sports, plus the animals and code to play them with. Always honor the man who goes abroad to find us new blood. Especially when he does it without two red cents in his pocket.

And finally we meet that concept again: versatility. The do-it-all dog. A hunter's single dog that can do it all, yet fit into an apartment, in this case, and ride in a Suzuki. Plus, and I haven't mentioned this before in this book, but as I make my rounds for *Field & Stream* and ask hunters, "Why did you choose this particular species of gun dog?" they all answer the same way.

THE FAMILY DOG

They say, "Because this breed makes such fine family dogs." Not that the dog is an accomplished and frenzied hunter, or once fetched a bear, or can ride on my front bumper and smell coon in the next county . . . but "this dog makes the best family pet." So you must factor that into the versatile dog selection as well.

And what these men and women are recognizing is the dog is hunted

Two cockers tell the cleric, "That bird is mine." And they mean it. Walt's cockers are birdy. (Photo by David Williams)

but three months out of the year, but he's underfoot in the kitchen the other 270 days.

Well, this book is done. But it could jell our minds to have some sort of review. So let's turn to the addendum.

But before going there let me say one last word about the Reverend Walt Cline. You'll never know the sacrifices he's made for cockerdom, for dogdom. He recently told me he gave a pup to a man interested in promoting the breed. This past weekend that man and that dog won a field trial in Denver. When Walt started saving the cocker there was no field trial for them in America. Because of Walt, more than any other man I know of, the cocker is alive and well in America and coursing the bird fields.

I give you Walt's address so you can write and express your gratitude. Contact Walt at 912 Box Butte Avenue, Alliance, Nebraska 69301.

Addendum

Lee Marvin had his "Dirty Dozen." I have my "Enlightened Nineteen," and one revisited. Doesn't mean these are all of the sensitive and humane gun dog trainers in America. It just means these are the nineteen I know. There has to be more, and in the future, I assure you there will be. This is a trend that can't be stopped for its time has come; we have the dogs to make it possible, and the trainers who'll do it no other way. It's an old saying, "Every dog has his day." Now, all dogs are going to have theirs. I've campaigned for humane training twenty years, and I thank all of you who have put your resolve into the same dream. You, who have made the dream an everyday way of training in America.

We don't need to review our tenets, our standard. We all know what they are. And many of you will be adding planks—good planks—of your own. For this humane gun dog training movement is young. And there is lots of room for innovation.

It just takes a kind heart. That's all. It just means you must intend to love the dog as much as you intend to use him. Why beat a dog to performance when you can smile him to it?

Of course—and this one reality stops many present trainers—you have to be smarter than the dog. And many trainers aren't. Your cue to this group is all those torture devices you see hanging in the back of their pickups.

Have you noticed how educated and wise, how vocal and discerning, each of the trainers was in this book? I have. These people aren't the prototype dog trainer. These people are canine scholars: they know their dogs, their educational process, their psyche, their uniqueness, and their genius. Yes, dogs are geniuses. That's what the new trainer must confess. And he must recognize the genius in order to confess it.

DOGS READ OUR MINDS

Dogs read our minds. Think not, then read my book, *The Magic of Dogs*. Dogs are clairvoyant, they are psychic, they are observers and interpreters of nuances in human behavior, they have a nose that can smell our mind-set.

Don't ever forget Web, the miracle retriever, who belongs to Mike Gould. Web can be a hill away and know every move Mike makes.

And pay attention to this. I've got four decades in the field of gun dogs, and two more than that just with coax-home dogs of my youth. And I want you to know this eternal truth. Remember when Wehle said, "I don't want a dog eighteen months old that's still a pup." Remember? And he furthermore said, "I pick a pup for intelligence."

Okay, what this means is this: *All dogs do not have the intelligence to detect human cues. Which means they cannot bond. So you must have this: a bright dog for a tight bond. Remember this, more than anything else. A bright dog for a tight bond.*

I have a houseful of dogs, and we live as one. One heart, one mind, one soul, one intent—that's what "bonded" means. The result is these dogs know what I'm going to do—before I do. Not that all of them are that bright; they're not. But the bright dogs decipher me, and the lesser-gifted decipher the bright ones. For dogs are uncanny at reading dogs.

Dogs are phenomenal. And to think they lived ten thousand years as "dumb beasts" in the eyes of insensitive humans.

WHO'S DUMB NOW

And now that we discover they ain't dumb at all, then who was?

So give the dog the benefit of the doubt. He's undoubtedly right. And I'm sure he's more forgiving than you.

You expect him to listen to you—well, listen back. You expect him to adhere to your nature—well, consider his. You expect him to love you—well, what's stopping you from reaching out?

Remember, a dog has all the virtues God said man should have—and doesn't. It's time we all started to live like a dog.

Index

About the Author

Bill Tarrant is the author of ten books on dogs and has been the gun dog editor for *Field & Stream* magazine since 1973. He has been named Writer of the Year by the Outdoor Writers Association of America, the Purina corporation, and the Dog Writers Association of America, the latter honoring him with the award twice. He has also received the Orvis Award for Distinguished Outdoor Literature. A former mayor of Wichita, Kansas, and a former professor of journalism at Wichita State University, Bill now makes his home in Las Vegas with his wife, Dee.